Narrating our Healing

Narrating our Healing
Perspectives on Working through Trauma

By

Chris N van der Merwe
&
Pumla Gobodo-Madikizela

CAMBRIDGE SCHOLARS PUBLISHING

Narrating our Healing: Perspectives on Working through Trauma, by Chris N van der Merwe and Pumla Gobodo-Madikizela

This book first published 2008 by

Cambridge Scholars Publishing

15 Angerton Gardens, Newcastle, NE5 2JA, UK

British Library Cataloguing in Publication Data
A catalogue record for this book is available from the British Library

ISBN (10): 1-84718-481-2, ISBN (13): 9781847184818

TABLE OF CONTENTS

Preface

The inspiration for this book comes, firstly, from the many conversations we have had together and with others over a three year period. In our discussions we have tried to deepen our understanding of the effects of massive trauma on individuals and on communities, of how people register the unspeakable traumas they have been exposed to in their lives, how they remember, and the tendency for traumatic memory to intrude unremittingly in the lives of victims and perpetrators. We feel privileged to have witnessed the working of the Truth and Reconciliation Commission (TRC) and to be able to draw from the insights of that important historical moment in South Africa.

One of the critical lessons we draw from the TRC is the lesson of hope: that in a country like ours, with a horrendous history of fierce racial divisions and gruesome stories of human rights abuses, it is possible to engage with and to be in peaceful human dialogue with one's former adversaries. Ordinary people, under certain circumstances, are capable, it transpires, of far greater evil than we would have imagined. But they are, too, capable of far greater virtue than we might have expected. Our humanity is strongest when we are led by the compassion that unites us as human beings. The TRC paved the way for us to the road that leads to a more humane humanity.

The second inspiration for this project was a course we offered at the University of Cape Town Summer School in 2004. The course was called "Narrative, Trauma, and Forgiveness". The class was a diverse group of about a hundred mature students from various disciplines who came from around the country, mostly from Cape Town and other parts of the Western Cape region. Ten years after the first democratic elections, and with the recent publication of its final amnesty report still a fresh memory, the TRC was a daily backdrop to our class discussions. Our classes during the week-long summer course became a place of engaging and stimulating intellectual discussion about trauma, narrative, and the various representational forms of traumatic memory. The discussions, however, went beyond the intellectual to a level of dialogue dealing with the question of what memory about "the past" means for us as South Africans with a range of experiences of that past, and differing identifications with it.

An extraordinary thing happened at the end of the summer class; people did not want to stop the dialogue. The class had run its course, but people expressed a desire to continue talking with one another. We made a special request to the organisers of the Summer School who moved us to another room, where dialogue continued. This was not the usual intellectual class discussion that is a natural part of university lecturing. The conversation was happening at a much deeper level with a richness of narrative and profound emotional engagement that we had not seen in our classes before. It seemed to us that what was unfolding was an important moment of witnessing; we were bearing witness to the memory that people carried about the past and their struggle with it.

The experience of massive trauma, such as the trauma associated with gross human rights abuses, usually overwhelms an individual and evokes a range of complex responses aimed at self-preservation. The experience of trauma impairs the capacity to register events fully as they occurred. The ability to integrate the objective events with the affective component of the experience is lost. Trauma has been described as the "undoing of the self", and as loss: loss of control, loss of one's identity, loss of the ability to remember, and loss of language to describe the horrific events.

The struggle with trauma is a struggle with memory. It is common for traumatised people to be confronted with painful traumatic memories long after the traumatic event occurred. Trauma is not remembered in the same way as normal events, but is often relived as flashbacks, as if it were recurring in the present. This is because, unlike normal events which are easily integrated into mental life, traumatic events are not easily assimilated. The repetitive intrusion of traumatic memory into the lives of survivors renders victims and survivors powerless, without any internal resources to control the intrusive traumatic memories.

Traumatic events, especially if they remain unacknowledged, continue to disempower victims, and intensify the feelings of shame and humiliation that are part of the legacy of trauma and its internalisation. This "internal" dimension of trauma is an important one: while the source of trauma may be external, the recurrent effects of trauma, and the impairment of the memory function—the "unfinished business" of trauma—are primarily reflections of an inner breakdown of the self and of an inner emotional conflict. The intrusive memories and the re-experiencing of trauma are the most distressing features of the aftermath of trauma. Victims and perpetrators of trauma feel helpless and at the mercy of the intrusive and fragmentary memories of trauma, unable to control these memories and completely victimised by them. Thus, healing of trauma, that is, the restoration of the self and the reclaiming of one's sense of control of memory, of the capacity to reflect, understand, and to perceive things as they are or were, requires transformation of traumatic memory into narrative memory.

Paul Ricœur and many other philosophers have shown us that we tend to regard our lives as narratives, with a beginning, middle and end. Some events seem insignificant to us and are forgotten, while others take a central place in the story we create from our lives. Life takes on the form of a plot with causal links, where one event leads to another—a plot that can, to a certain extent, be planned by us, the authors of our own lives. Trauma, however, destroys the belief that we are in control of our lives; it leaves us shattered and powerless. This book deals with the process of regaining control; it is about the search for meaning after trauma and the rewriting of life's narrative to incorporate the catastrophe.

In the first chapter, various meanings of the two key concepts in this book, "narrative" and "healing", are explored. "Narrative" could refer to the narrative structure that we confer on our lives, or the communal narratives created by a nation or an ethnic group, or to individual narratives about personal experiences, or to the narratives of Literature. "Healing", we will argue, does not imply an end to all pain and suffering, but rather facing and work through trauma, so that the tragic loss caused by trauma is balanced by a gain in meaning. On this issue, our arguments are linked to Viktor Frankl's plea for a "tragic optimism".

Trauma victims have a contradictory desire to suppress their trauma as well as to talk about it. To talk about it, would mean an extremely painful reliving of the event—so, for inner survival, they normally suppress the memory. Yet, paradoxically, it is precisely confrontation of the suppressed memory that is needed for inner healing. Instead of working through trauma, victims of trauma typically re-enact it, but with a reversal of roles: with themselves as perpetrator, where they have the power and are in control, so that they can transfer their revenge onto a new victim. This reaction to trauma can often lead to an endless repetition of violence: at either individual or communal level. It is vital that both perpetrators and victims should transcend their respective roles; that they be reconciled and start exploring their common humanity. The tension between silence and disclosure, and ways of working through trauma are the central themes of chapter 2.

A large part of chapter 3, entitled "Searching for Closure: The Crying Voice", contains a traumatic story where closure keeps evading the victims. The crying voice referred to could be seen as a symbolic representative of the many crying voices from South Africa's traumatic past, searching for attention and closure. One of the ways of dealing with these voices is then discussed in the chapter, namely to make public spaces intimate, to share stories by people from different backgrounds and histories. In this process of reconciliation, forgiveness plays a crucial role—it liberates both the victim and the perpetrator and opens up the way to a future free from the divisions of the past.

The links between literary narratives and trauma are discussed in chapter 4. Since trauma is characterised by a loss of plot, the traumatic experience cannot be immediately "translated" into the narrative structures of our mental memory; therefore, according to Ernst van Alphen, trauma signifies a "failed experience". However, literary writers invent new narratives through which the traumatic memory of readers can be vicariously expressed, so that they can experience a catharsis. Literary narratives can help us to confront our traumas, to bring to light what has been suppressed; it also imagines new possibilities of living meaningfully in a changed world.

However, the reading of literature should not be seen as a "quick fix" for trauma. The healing process is a complex, continuing process. We cannot prescribe one book that would provide a general cure for trauma: one and the same book could be harmful to one reader and meaningful to another, and the same book could have different effects at different stages of a person's life. Books are like friends, they have to be chosen carefully according to the individual traits and circumstances of a specific reader. We do not, of course, advocate reading innocuous narratives with happy endings to console traumatised readers; on the contrary, such stories would not ring true and could actually aggravate the trauma. On the other hand, gruelling stories could provide some kind of consolation for a trauma sufferer who finds validation for her own experience in the narrative.

The healing potential of literary narratives can be seen from the point of the writer, who could find a catharsis through the (indirect) expression of suppressed pain, or from the viewpoint of the reader, who could find some kind of healing through discovering points of identification residing in the narrative. There is certainly room for the study of the connection between the writing of stories and the healing of the psyche, but we will focus here on the reader's side in the literary communication, on the dialogue between text and reader. Thus in the last chapter of this book, the novel *Disgrace* by J M Coetzee is examined as an example of a literary narrative about traumatic phenomena and ways of working through them. Many people have found *Disgrace* a disturbing text and would be surprised at the choice of this book to conclude our discussion on narratives of healing. Yet the novel brings together many of the threads in this book: the loss of plot and the rewriting of one's life narrative; the creation of new communal narratives in South Africa; the role of forgiveness in bridging the divides in the country; and last but not least, the importance of the great "archetypes of the mind", the ethical concepts without which individuals and societies would fall apart.

In this book, we advocate collaboration between the disciplines of psychology and literature, to examine jointly the nature of trauma and ways of dealing with it. In studying relevant literary texts, scholars of literature and psychology can complement each other in understanding thoughts and emotions embedded in the text and their relevance to trauma. Literary texts can also be used by therapists to facilitate discussion on trauma and help the patient to work through it. This kind of cooperation between scholars from psychology and literature is, obviously, not the only way to approach literature or deal with trauma, but it could prove fruitful to both disciplines.

Other forms of narrative art could also be used in working through trauma. The narratives told in film, drama, video and television could be extremely helpful in dealing with trauma; also, in a different way, fine art and music contain narratives of trauma. But that is material for another book.

Events like rape and bodily assault, earthquakes and floods, are clearly traumatic in nature. However, we would argue that trauma is not restricted to these extreme events. If trauma is seen as the shattering of a life narrative, it is an experience common to all. We all know of shattered dreams, of life treating us contrary to our desires; we know of illness and the death of loved ones. Therefore we will also deal with this more “everyday” appearance of trauma, with the search for meaning familiar to all people.

The theme of this book, namely the importance of narration for the healing of trauma, has had a marked influence on its form. After the explication in chapter 1 of concepts central in our argumentation, narratives seep into the arguments more and more. Chapter 2 contains two stories; a large part of chapter 3 is a story; chapter 4 begins and ends with a narrative; and chapter 5 contains an analysis of a literary narrative. Stories illuminate key issues and central ideas explored in the book. Often, we have found, narratives are more effective in conveying the complexities of trauma than rational argument. Our topic has greatly determined the style and structure of our book.

Democracy has been with us in South Africa for twelve years now. Yet the ghosts of the past have not been laid to rest, at least not completely, and new challenges lie ahead. The task of putting together the pieces of a society shattered by violence is not easy. Reconciliation cannot be condensed into a quick project, it needs consistent work, on a personal and on a public level. Perhaps the most enduring effects of totalitarian rule and the systematic oppression under apartheid cannot be measured in terms of the numbers dead, but in immeasurable losses of the human spirit. That is what has to be restored.

It is our sincere hope that this book will make a meaningful contribution to the discussion of a topic that will continue to challenge our country and our world in the years ahead: how to narrate our healing.

University of Cape Town
February 2007

CHAPTER ONE

LIFE AS A NARRATIVE

Life in search of a narrative

"Stories are told and not lived; life is lived and not told." This sounds like common sense; and yet, says the French philosopher Paul Ricœur, it is only partially true (Ricœur 1991: 425). For stories are also lived, and life is told. The point that stories are lived, is the topic of chapter 4; the topic of this chapter is the transformation of our lives into stories.

Ricœur finds in human experience a "pre-narrative quality"; he sees life as "an incipient story … *an activity and a desire in search of a narrative*". [All quoted emphasis is original unless noted otherwise.] He suggests that we tend to "see a certain chain of episodes in our lives as *stories not yet told,* stories that seek to be told" (434). We tend not to leave daily experiences "as they are", but to examine and interpret them, to link them to one another. Socrates asserted that the unexamined life is not worth living. Ricœur agrees, but says, in addition, that to examine a life means turning it into a narrative: "Socrates's life examined is a life *narrated*" (435).

For most of us, our experience does not consist of unrelated elements; present, past and future seem to be intertwined. Alasdair MacIntyre talks of "the unity of a narrative which links birth to life to death as a narrative [links] beginning to middle to end" (MacIntyre 1981: 191). However, it must be emphasised that we have a choice about the nature of the narratives into which we transform our lives. Narrating a life means becoming the author of one's life. Although one cannot control the events in one's life completely, one has a choice how to interpret the data of one's life and how to act on the basis of that interpretation. Although we cannot absorb the overwhelming amount of information within and about us, we can distinguish between the significant and the insignificant and, led by that distinction, decide on our future actions. Like authors, who create narratives by selecting and structuring life's data, we too can turn our experience into narratives, as is explained by Willie Burger:

> We are always planning for the future and reviewing the past. Therefore we are always, in the light of our future plans and our past experience, busy selecting

> certain sensory data and ignoring other information. In this sense we are always narrating our own lives (selecting and structuring information), not only after actions and events, but also while we are acting and experiencing. My actions are the result of my plans for the future and my story of my past experience. (Burger 2001: 83)

We are the narrators of our life stories, and we also play the part of the main character in them—therefore our stories are "autobiographies", unified by the actions of a main character striving towards a future and determined by a past. Furthermore, not only are we the narrators of our lives and the main characters of our stories, but we are also the "readers" of our lives. Like the readers of a literary story, we search for links between the different events of our lives. In "reading" our lives, we use techniques similar to those of a literary reader; we move from specific scenes to general themes, and from the general back to the specific.

Turning one's life into a narrative is a vital way of finding meaning: in discovering causal links between different events we create a coherent *plot* from our lives which leads to an understanding of how "things fit together". 'Emplotment' is a way of creating coherence in the seemingly confusing course of our lives. We examine our lives to find central *themes* and *patterns* which permeate our diverse experiences—patterns which could make sense of life as a variety of "enactments" of recurrent themes. The discovery of a plot and of recurring thematic patterns enables us to distinguish between the significant and the insignificant. Significant events are those that have a strong influence on the plot and form part of fundamental patterns in the narrative.

Transforming the events in one's life into a narrative structure is a way of counteracting the transience of life. In a narrative, every small component forms part of the whole: when one episode has been narrated, it is not over, because it keeps reverberating, influencing the rest of the plot, commenting on central themes and reflecting the values incorporated in the rest of the story. Every part is reflected in the whole, and vice versa.

Narration confers identity on the narrated life. The writings of Paul Ricœur are full of insight on this topic. In his discussion of the concept of "narrative identity", he distinguishes between two Latin words for identity: *idem* and *ipse. Idem* refers to an abstract, formal identity, *ipse* to a dynamic identity; *idem* refers to that which is always exactly the same; *ipse* on the other hand is "self-sameness", constancy within a variety of circumstances—it is a "narrative identity" which creates cohesion within a life which would otherwise fall apart. "Self-sameness, 'self-constancy' (*ipse*), can escape the dilemma of the Same and the Other to the extent that its identity rests on a temporal structure that conforms to the model of a dynamic identity arising from the poetic composition of a narrative text … Unlike the abstract identity of the Same (*idem*), this narrative identity, constitutive of self-constancy, can include change, mutability, within the cohesion of one lifetime" (Ricœur 1988: 246).

From the above it becomes clear that narrative identity involves a willingness to take responsibility for one's own life, an ethical choice to remain constant.

> Self-constancy is for each person that manner of conducting himself or herself so that others can *count on* that person. Because someone is counting on me, I am *accountable for* my actions before another. The term 'responsibility' unites both meanings: 'counting on' and 'being accountable for'. It unites them, adding to them the idea of a *response* to the question: 'Where are you?' asked by another who needs me. This response is the following: 'Here I am!' a response that is a statement of constancy. (Ricœur 1992: 165)

The development of life's narrative is fundamentally directed by the ethical values of the narrator; if there is constancy in the ethics, it provides coherence to the narrative. At the end of one's life, one's narrative is a storehouse of ethical choices and values, and the value of one's past life is determined by the values incorporated in it. The idea of turning one's life into a narrative is deeply involved with the question of what the best kind of life is. Ricœur says: "The idea of gathering together one's life in the form of a narrative is destined to serve as a basis for the aim of a 'good' life, the cornerstone of (our) ethics". (Ricœur 1992: 158). For him, the highest possible goal is "*aiming at the 'good life' with and for others, in just institutions*" (172).

The creation of a narrative from the data of our lives does not mean that we can ever completely comprehend the meaning of our lives. We are still in the midst of our stories, striving towards a desired end. We do not know what will happen to us, we do not understand why everything that has happened has happened to us; much darkness envelops us. Even at the end of our lives, a full understanding will still elude us. So, narrating our lives does not mean to come to a full understanding of life, but rather to strive towards a meaningful existence and to live the best of possible lives.

Different meanings of the narration of life—the communal aspect

We should distinguish between different meanings of the concept of "life narrative". It can refer to the structure that I have consciously conferred on to my life, but it is possible that I have suppressed traumatic aspects of my life into the subconscious mind, so that the actual narrative of my life encompasses much more than the narrative I have consciously formed; it also includes the personal subconscious mind, the trauma that I have failed to confront. Ideally, everyone should go through a process that Jung called "individuation", that is, becoming "a separate, indivisible unity or 'whole'"; a process in which consciousness and unconsciousness become integrated (Jung 1968: 275). "Consciousness should defend its reason and protect itself, and the chaotic life of the unconscious should be given the chance of having its way too—as much of it as we can stand. This means open conflict and open collaboration at once. That, evidently, is what human life should be" (288). When this happens, the narrative of my life reflects an inner wholeness, an integration of the conscious and the subconscious mind.

The narrative of my life is linked to a multitude of other narratives, and its interaction with these other narratives forms part of its total meaning. Narrating my life is not merely an individual matter. I am not only the main character of my own story, but also a minor character in the stories of others; my story is intertwined with those of others. My story is embedded in family histories and in the history of a city and a country; *my* story is part of *our* story. David Carr puts it as follows:

> To inhabit a territory, to organise politically and economically for its cultivation and civilisation, to experience a natural or human threat and rise to meet it—these are experiences and actions usually not properly attributable to me alone, or to me, you and the others individually. They belong rather to us: it is not my experience but *ours,* not I who act but *we* who act in concert. (Carr 1997: 18)

We inherit a communal past from our families, cities, countries; it is never possible to make a completely "new beginning". According to Alasdair MacIntyre, the legacy from the past constitutes

> the given of my life, my moral starting point … I am born with a past; and to try to cut myself off from that past, in the individualistic mode, is to deform my present relationships. The possession of an historical identity and the possession of a social identity coincide. Notice that rebellion against my identity is always one possible mode of expressing it. (MacIntyre 1981: 205)

Communities and nations also narrate their past; they create histories (stories!), with heroes and villains, to make sense of their present and guide them into the future. We form—to use the title of Benedict Anderson's influential book—"imagined communities". In divided countries, different stories are made of the same historic material. Thus, in South Africa, the struggle from the 1950s to 1990 was called, on the one hand, a liberation struggle against the racist oppression of the apartheid regime, and, on the other hand, those in power spread the narrative of a struggle to protect the country's civilised, Christian values against the onslaught of Communist terrorists.

We are born into stories, and have no choice in that matter—in a fundamental way, they determine our identities. Yet I do have a choice about my *position* in relation to the conventional narratives; I can decide on points of identification in the transmitted stories. In the interaction between individual and collective narratives, the personal identity is continually created and recreated. Stuart Hall puts it as follows: "Cultural identities are the points of identification, the unstable points of identification or suture, which are made with the discourse of history and culture. Not an essence but a *positioning*" (Hall 1994: 395).

The narrative that I form from my experience is my legacy to the community and to the world. In a famous Dutch poem, "Oinou hena stalagmon", J H Leopold poetically describes a drop of wine flowing from a bottle broken on the prow of a ship to ensure a safe journey. (The meaning of the Greek title is "A drop of wine".) The drop falling into the ocean is absorbed in the sea water; mixing with the ocean, it gradually spreads itself, until its influence is felt, in a new equilibrium, throughout the enormous expanse of water. This, for Leopold, is an image of the wide-spread influence that can flow from one powerful thought of a poet.

Not all of us are poets, but as narrators of our lives something akin to poetry emerges within us. My small narrative is submerged in larger narratives, where it exerts a never-ending influence. My life influences those who come into contact with me, but it does not stop there; in an ever-spreading influence, like ripples caused by a stone thrown into a dam, my narrative spreads further, from those in contact with me to those in contact with them, in a never-ending movement. The effects brought about by my narrative change the present and can open up new possibilities for the future. Even the past is not left unchanged. Cartoon character Charlie Brown said, "What I am hoping for is a better yesterday"; and my narrative may do just that, because by being linked to the narratives of the past it may give a new significance to them. For instance: the achievements of Nelson Mandela give a great significance to the lives of his parents (and to their parents, and so on.) I am not Nelson Mandela, but even my small narrative, like Leopold's drop of wine, has a greater influence on present, past and future than I may realise. It is impossible to cancel that influence. Even people committing suicide, pronouncing the death sentence on themselves and cutting themselves off from the world create a legacy of grief; even the person living in isolation is not without effect, because the isolation creates a vacuum, a gap which affects others who might otherwise have been in touch with that life. Ultimately, my choice is not between narrating my life and not narrating it, but between creating a good, bad or indifferent narrative. "He who has been, from then on cannot not have been: henceforth this mysterious and profoundly obscure fact of having been is his viaticum for all eternity" (Vladimir Jankélévitch – quoted as motto in Ricœur 2004).

Trauma and life narratives

Narrating one's life is about finding structure, coherence and meaning in life. Trauma, in contrast, is about the shattering of life's narrative structure, about a loss of meaning—the traumatised person has "lost the plot". A fundamental issue concerning trauma is the regaining of meaning after trauma, the rewriting of one's life narrative to incorporate the traumatic loss in the new narrative. Ricœur mentions the duty of the psychiatrist, when someone comes to him or her with the "bits and pieces" of a broken life story, to help the patient to recreate it into "a story that is both more intelligible and more bearable" (Ricœur 1991: 435). Typically, victims of trauma, when relating the experience, begin with the time before the trauma. For them, a crucial matter is the abyss between the time before and after the trauma, an abyss that has destroyed all feelings of continuity and order, and they need to include the abyss in their story. Overwhelming trauma is like an earthquake, wiping out the world as it was known; and the daunting challenge is to build a new narrative that connects the trauma with the life coming before and after it.

Extreme trauma leads to a loss of words, because language is insufficient to describe the experience. Charlotte Delbo (1990: 3–4) distinguishes between "intellectual/external memory" and "deep memory". Intellectual memory can be verbalised; deep memory cannot, because the language has been torn apart by trauma:

> Deep memory preserves sensations, physical imprints. It is the memory of the senses. For it isn't words that are swollen with emotional charge. Otherwise, someone who has been tortured by thirst for weeks on end could never again say 'I'm thirsty. How about a cup of tea.' The word has also split in two. *Thirst* has turned back into a word for commonplace use. But if I dream of the thirst I suffered in Birkenau, I once again see the person I was, haggard, halfway crazed, near to collapse; I physically feel that real thirst and it is an atrocious nightmare.

Therefore, although she knows for a fact that she was in the concentration camp at Birkenau, she cannot recall it in everyday language, because the language is insufficient—therefore "I no longer know if it is real" (Delbo 1990: 3–4). In chapter 4, we examine how Delbo uses literary techniques and language to express her traumatic experience. Not only does everyday language seem incapable of expressing trauma, but talking about trauma leads to the reliving of the traumatic event. That is why there are conflicting desires in traumatised persons—they want to talk about their trauma to work through it, but they also want to suppress it into the subconscious and conceal it—which is the topic of chapter 2.

At this stage it is necessary to make further distinctions between the ways in which the word "narrative" is being used here. "Narratives" can refer to literary narratives; it can also refer to autobiographical stories, stories in which people tell what happened to them (like Charlotte Delbo telling of her life in Auschwitz). Furthermore, "narrative" can be used figuratively, as Ricœur uses it, to describe the search for coherence and meaning in one's life—the desire to transform one's life into a "plot". Although one should distinguish between the different usages of the word, they are all linked to the creation of coherence and meaning. Language is of fundamental importance in all the usages, for when life's narrative is destroyed by trauma, it leads to a loss of words, an inability to narrate a central episode in one's life; and finding the language to narrate is vital for the refiguration of one's life narrative.

Fitting the pieces together is not only an issue for individuals, but for societies too. In her book *A Human Being Died That Night*, Pumla Gobodo-Madikizela tells of her interviews with Eugene de Kock—"Prime Evil" of the apartheid era. It is the story of two people from opposing life narratives, with opposite views of right and wrong and of heroes and villains, who get together and discover a common humanity. That, on a micro scale, suggests a way for the reconciliation of a nation. The book also discusses the importance of forgiveness in bridging the divisions between the victims and the perpetrators of the past.

We mentioned that conflicting narratives have been told of South Africa's history preceding the first fully democratic election in 1994—on the one hand, it was regarded as a struggle for freedom from racist oppression, on the other hand as a combat against terrorists threatening civilisation. Both these narratives lost their meaning in 1994, when the armed struggle ended and the need for the building of a new society arose. Apart from being traumatised by apartheid, South Africa is at present a country traumatised in another sense: the loss of guiding narratives has left a void in its wake. Political and religious leaders have made efforts to fill the emptiness and new narratives have emerged, narratives about the "rainbow nation" and the "African Renaissance".

Writers, who have the necessary imagination and the power of words, could play a key role in the creation of new narratives: by questioning existing narratives, where necessary, and imagining new stories to live by. The role of literary narratives in the healing of a nation is the topic of chapters 4 and 5.

The Lamentation of Job

A natural tendency, for individuals and for communities, is to turn their present and past into sentimental, romantic stories with reassuring conclusions. We like to believe the best about ourselves—maybe a flaw or two, but "our hearts are in the right place". We like to believe that life is good: people are basically benevolent, and justice will ultimately prevail; we like to agree with Robert Browning: "God's in his heaven, all's right with the world". But trauma fundamentally challenges these assumptions.

Perhaps the most famous example in world literature of this kind of challenge is to be found in the Book of Job. Job's life narrative initially made total sense: he was a good man and was justly rewarded by God for his goodness: he was healthy and wealthy, and his good fortune was shared by his large family. Not only was Job "blameless and upright" but, to be completely on the safe side, he also regularly made sacrifices to God for the sake of his children, in case they had, without his knowledge, sinned against God. Not a finger could be pointed at him, and yet, out of the blue, he loses his children, his wealth and his health—and with this trauma, he loses the basis of his life narrative: the belief that goodness is rewarded and evil punished.

These events are told in the first two chapters of the Book of Job; after that, in the next forty chapters, the fundamental questions flowing from the calamity are faced, when three of Job's friends (later also a fourth one) turn up and argue about the reasons for Job's sudden misfortune. There are a number of points emanating from this text which are relevant to our discussion of life narratives and trauma:

1. When the friends arrive at Job's home, they preserve seven days of silence. They have the wisdom to realise that, after experiencing intense pain, one does not want to talk about it straight away; it is too painful. They understand that what Job needs at this moment is to have sympathetic friends who are willing to sit with him quietly and patiently, sharing his pain. They know that great trauma leads to a loss of words.

2. After this promising start, the friends become less understanding. Job breaks the silence by cursing the day of his birth and blaming God for his misfortune. To his friends, this is blasphemous, and they regard it as their duty to defend the Name of God. God is a just God, they maintain, and if bad things happened to Job, he must have done bad things that offended God. This reveals the crux of their own life narrative—a narrative that has given them security, one that they do not dare to let go of. They do not realise that they are merely offering Job's shattered life narrative back to him—the narrative based on the belief that God is just, that He rewards goodness and punishes badness. Instead of opening their minds up to Job's real calamity—the loss of a life narrative—

they force their own life narrative on to him, a narrative that, in Job's experience, has proved to be false.

3. The friends nonetheless play a positive role in Job's dealing with his trauma. They serve as a sounding board and provide him with an opportunity to express his pain and vent his anger; actions which are essential before he can ultimately find peace.

4. Job never comes to a complete understanding of why he was struck by calamity. The dialogue between God and Satan, their decision to test the virtue of Job (in chapters 1 and 2) takes place before the throne of God, so that Job knows nothing about the heavenly agreement preceding his misfortune. At the end of the story, God makes His appearance and addresses Job and his friends; but He never justifies His ways to Job, He only reminds Job of the greatness of creation and, by implication, of its Creator. God puts Job in his place, reminding him that, from a Godly perspective, he is a minute creature, created by the self-same God whom he has dared to accuse. Job then finds peace in the acknowledgement that he is not God's equal and has no right to blame God or demand justification of His ways.

5. After Job's magnificent accusations of God, bravely asking the questions that no-one else dares to ask, this resignation comes as an anti-climax. But there is another turn in the discussion: surprisingly, God commends Job for the harsh way in which he spoke about Him, and condemns his friends for their incorrect way of speaking about God (Job 42 v 7). God values Job's sincere, brave speaking of his mind, and dislikes the friends' "justification" of God with their naive assumptions. God appreciates Job's faith, which has gone through a period of deep and honest doubt, and survived.

6. The Book of Job has a "happy ending". Job gets back more than he possessed before calamity struck: increased wealth and offspring, and health. In a way, the ending runs contrary to the fundamental idea of the book: that good people are *not* always rewarded with prosperity. Also, one could question the implication that Job was completely recompensed for his original losses: although he had other children, those who died were irrevocably lost. However, one should not overlook what is perhaps the most crucial aspect of the "happy ending", which goes beyond the naive idea that the just will be rewarded with prosperity: the fact that Job's circumstances were changed *when he prayed for his friends* (Job 42: 10). Having worked through his personal grief, he is no longer enveloped in his own trauma, and is able to look at his friends with empathy and care. The good man is rewarded with goodness.

7. Even more important than Job's finding of peace, is the fact that the trauma of Job is the thematic material that leads to the creation of a literary masterpiece. Trauma may be a stimulus for the creation of art. "The wound is a talking mouth", says one of the characters in Etienne van Heerden's novel

Kikuyu (Van Heerden 1998: 153). In the "Afterword" to his two books on his Holocaust experience, *If This is a Man* and *The Truce*, Primo Levi says:

> If I had not lived the Auschwitz experience, I probably would never have written anything … [O]nto my brief and tragic experience as a deportee has been overlaid that much longer and complex experience of writer-witness, and the sum total is clearly positive: in its totality, this past has made me richer and surer. (Levi n.d.: 397–398)

Trauma does often lead to the expression and narration of pain. This not only applies to writers like Primo Levi or the author of the Book of Job; it can also be true of all people going through trauma and rethinking their life narratives. Trauma may lead to the re-imagining of conventional narratives, the creative "rewriting" of one's life story to make it uniquely one's own.

We have brought together the lives of ordinary people and of a literary character like Job; we have linked the re-creation of life narratives with literary narratives. That is not surprising, since a basic assumption of this book is the connection between trauma and language. Trauma means a loss of language, we have maintained; creating or re-creating a life narrative means that one has a story that can be narrated. When one struggles with a shattered life story, literary narratives can help to find words for one's trauma, as will be discussed more elaborately in chapters 4 and 5.

The Book of Job contains the *laments* of Job, and the genre of the lament is a valuable vehicle to help ordinary people with the expression of trauma. Denise Ackermann writes about the ways in which the language of lament can be used for the expression of a wide spectrum of human emotions. According to her, lament

> is a coil of suffering and hope, awareness and memory, anger and relief, a desire for vengeance, forgiveness, and healing that beats against the heart of God. It is our way of bearing the unbearable … It is, in essence, supremely human. (Ackermann 2003: 111)

> Lament is like a hot poultice applied to a festering boil. At first it is painful; it burns, and one application does not do the trick. Gradually, the inflammation becomes localised, the poultice draws the pus out, the angry redness subsides, the pain is relieved and healing begins. (121)

Two kinds of trauma

Before we continue our argument, we should distinguish between two kinds of trauma, as Dominick LaCapra (1991) does:

(a) *historical trauma*, which refers to a single huge disaster, which can be personal (for instance, a rape) or communal (like a flood);

(b) *structural trauma*, which refers to a pattern of continual and continuing traumas.

It is interesting to note that people suffering from structural trauma may gradually become so used to the traumatic situation that it becomes traumatic to move out of it; what most people call "normal" has become abnormal for them. In a lecture at the University of Cape Town, Valerie Sinason told of her experience as a young psychologist, when a girl who had been raped repeatedly, came to her consulting rooms. As she entered, the girl started taking off her clothes, ready to be raped. Sinason tried to console her, assuring her that the consulting room was different from her "normal" surroundings, that she was safe there. Then, surprisingly, all hell broke loose, because the girl was terrified by the thought of "normality".

Structural trauma and historical trauma are harmful in different ways. Structural trauma is not only painful in itself, but leaving the well-known framework of that situation may be—at least at first—even more painful; historical trauma, on the other hand, causes its pain by the shattering of a protective framework that had seemed so safe. Our discussion here will focus mainly on historical trauma, but it will also be related to the issue of structural trauma.

Disasters ingrained in life

It is necessary now to return to the fundamental question of the relation between trauma and life narratives. At the beginning of the twenty-first century, two disasters happened that dominated the news media for weeks: the fall of the Twin Towers in New York on 11 September 2001 and the tsunami disaster of 26 December 2004. In a dramatic way, these events remind us of the suffering caused by human inhumanity to other humans and by the destructive forces of nature. They both caused trauma on an enormous scale, with the tsunami killing hundreds of thousands of people, and both plunging even more people into deep mourning and leaving survivors with overwhelming, meaning-shattering memories.

Such disasters evoke age-old questions about the meaning of life. For believers in the providence of God, questions related to those asked by Job, arise: Does God really exist? If so, why did He allow this to happen? Why do the innocent have to suffer? Is God really in control of events? Why does God not control the forces of nature properly? Why does He not protect the innocent against the cruelties of the wicked? Is God maybe not almighty? Or worse, is God not benevolent? These terrible events can easily suggest that God is either not in control, or He is not good. God apparently transgresses against His own laws: according to tradition, God demands justice from humans and forbids them to commit cruelty and murder; but on a tremendous scale He seems to harm and kill people by fire and water, and through cruel human hands. Such events can shatter the framework of beliefs of those who believe that "God's in his heaven, all's right with the world", and lead to a severe loss of coherence in their lives.

Because of the enormity of disasters such as those mentioned above, we tend to regard them as exceptional events. We tend to say determinedly, especially after catastrophes due to human cruelty, such as the extinction of Jews by the Nazis: Never again! Yet the reality is: Yet again—alas! The end of the Second World War did not bring an end to human atrocities—in the next decades, they happened in Russia, southern Africa, Vietnam, Rwanda, and in many other places. Natural disasters like floods, earthquakes and fires continue to inflict suffering and death. In South Africa, according to UNAids, 456 000 people died of Aids in 2003—almost two tsunamis! Catastrophes on a huge scale, like the tsunami of 2004, are not as exceptional as they seem; they are like a magnifying glass that can help us to see the suffering that is ingrained in human life. Even people with calm and relatively predictable lives have to cope with the ubiquity and often the unexpectedness of death. Of course the fact that disasters have no end should not stop us from trying to remove and alleviate, as far as possible, the causes and effects of the catastrophes; but we should not allow ourselves to be placated with the hope that suffering can be removed from the world.

For Hindus, suffering is an inherent part of life. When a Hindu was asked to comment on the effect of the tsunami on his religious faith, he replied that the catastrophe was completely in accordance with his beliefs. The god Shiva in whom Hindus believe is both destructive and creative, and the symbolic dance of Shiva suggests the continual destruction as well as the continual renewal of the world; it indicates the inextricable intertwinement of life and death. And indeed, the tsunami was followed by new activity and restoration. The world's dormant compassion was awakened, and the ruined areas received food, clothes, money and assistance in abundance; old feuds were forgotten as people united to rebuild the devastated regions.

Frankl's search for meaning

This brings us to the crux of the topic explored in this chapter: the links between trauma and the search for meaning, between the shattering and recreating of life narratives. In 1945, after surviving the horrors of Auschwitz, Viktor Frankl wrote, in nine days, a book that would make him famous and would later be published in English under the title *Man's Search for Meaning.*

In the edition of 1984, a postscript was added: "The case for a tragic optimism". In reaction to his experiences in Auschwitz, Frankl expounds his views about *logotherapy*, a therapy based on the necessity of finding meaning in order to survive physically and mentally in the midst of severe suffering. Quoting Nietzsche, he maintains: "He who has a *why* to live for can bear with almost any *how*" (Frankl 1985: 97.

In his postscript of 1984, Frankl mentions the "tragic triad" that makes it difficult "to say yes to life", namely pain, guilt and death (161). He then discusses ways of finding meaning within the tragic triad, which make it possible to live with "tragic optimism", that is, with optimism in spite of the tragic aspects of life. He bases his theory on "the human capacity to creatively turn life's negative aspects into something positive or constructive". The tragic triad can be counteracted by: "(1) turning suffering into a human achievement and accomplishment; (2) deriving from guilt the opportunity to change oneself for the better; and (3) deriving from life's transitoriness an incentive to take responsible action." According to Frankl, "a human being is not one in pursuit of happiness but rather in search of a reason to become happy … through actualising the potential meaning inherent and dormant in a given situation" (162).

Frankl gives a number of examples of meaningful responses to suffering. Suffering may lead to meaningful action, for instance when a person who has recovered from a terminal illness starts helping others with a similar illness. (One could add many other examples of meaningful, active responses to suffering: to protest against human injustice, cruelty and violence; to support efforts to control the forces of nature; to alleviate the effects of a natural disaster by sending food and clothes to those in need, and so on.) Suffering, according to Frankl, may also enrich our existence through meaningful new encounters and relationships.

Of the utmost importance, furthermore, is the possibility for personal growth created by suffering—it can for instance lead to increased compassion and greater strength of character.

In accordance with our views on the importance of ethical values in life narratives, Frankl notes that our past always remains part of us, and its quality is determined by the values realised in it:

> Just as life remains potentially meaningful under any conditions, even those which are most miserable, so too does the value of each and every person stay with him or her, and it does so because it is based on the values that he or she has realized in the past. (1985: 176)

More important than the fact that we suffer, is the way in which we respond to suffering. Unlike Freud, Frankl notes great differences in our responses to it:

> Sigmund Freud once asserted, 'Let one attempt to expose a number of the most diverse people uniformly to hunger. With the increase of the imperative urge of hunger all individual differences will blur, and in their stead will appear the uniform expression of the one unstilled urge.' Thank heaven, Sigmund Freud was spared knowing the concentration camps from the inside. His subjects lay on a couch designed in the plush style of Victorian culture, not in the filth of Auschwitz. *There*, the 'individual differences' did *not* 'blur' but, on the contrary, people became more different; people unmasked themselves, both the swine and the saints. (178)

Frankl admits that the saints form a minority group, but he challenges his readers to join the minority, and warns them to be alert, because:

> "Since Auschwitz we know what man is capable of. And since Hiroshima we know what is at stake." (179)

Frankl's search for meaning does not imply that one can discover a final meaning that will last, unaltered, for the rest of one's life; neither does it suggest the possibility of finding a single, all-encompassing meaning which will provide the right answer to all life's problems and which is applicable, without adaptation, to all people. On the contrary, he says, "the meaning of life differs from man to man, from day to day and from hour to hour" (131–132). The search for meaning is never-ending, and it requires taking individual responsibility.

The search for meaning also does not imply that it is possible to reach a complete understanding of life with all its complexities and contradictions; its primary objective is not to find answers to questions such as: Who is to blame for my suffering? Did God plan it? Does my trauma fit into a greater scheme of things? Rather than looking from the trauma "backwards" and brooding over these unanswerable questions about the (human, heavenly or diabolical) causes of the suffering, Frankl points from the trauma forward, to the future, suggesting ways of responding to the trauma that may transform it from tragedy into a life-enriching experience. Ironically, by looking forward from the suffering to the future and not backwards in search of reasons for its happening, one may indeed, by one's creative response to a trauma, *create* a valid reason for its occurrence. In our terms, Frankl sees trauma as a stimulus to re-imagine one's life story; he suggests ways of recreating one's life narrative to incorporate the trauma; to create a narrative which will, when completed, be filled with value.

We have given much attention to Frankl's views because they are so relevant to our discussion. They are linked to issues discussed above—issues such as the ideals of leading the best of possible lives, of filling one's life with values, of finding coherence and continuity; the necessity of taking responsibility for one's life; and the connections between trauma and life narratives.

There is another link between Frankl's and our ideas, which is suggested by the name he gave to his theory: *logotherapy.* The Greek word "logos" to which the term refers, has various meanings: it means "word"; it can also mean "narrative"; furthermore, it can refer to order, it is linked to reason and logic—it is sometimes translated into Latin as "ratio". The fact that the word "logos" suggests a link between "word" and "narrative" on the one hand, and "order" and "logic" on the other hand, is no coincidence. In English similar links are found: the words "meaning" and "sense" refer to the communication through language (the *meaning* of words; talking *sense*) as well as to order and purpose in life (the *meaning* of life; making *sense* of what happened). Language and order are linked.

Trauma defies language; it resists being communicated. The recovery from trauma begins with the finding of words and of a story about what happened; "translating" trauma into the structure of a language and a narrative is a way of bringing order and coherence into the chaotic experience. Furthermore, trauma can be communicated and shared through language, which also helps the healing process. Frankl's logotherapy is a search for purpose *and* a search for words. According to Biblical tradition, in the beginning the earth was "without form and void", but when God *spoke*, order was created out of the chaos; similarly, the void created by trauma needs words to be transformed into something meaningful.

Objections to Frankl

Although we have indicated our agreement with many of Frankl's ideas, some objections could be raised against his views. People who are in shock after a trauma, do not want to hear that they must "pull themselves together" or "look on the bright side of things". They need a period of wordless mourning, of painful meditation on what happened, before they can move forward. Any talk about a search for meaning in suffering would be offensive to a traumatised person who is emotionally not ready for it. And even when the search for meaning begins, the journey often moves one or two steps forward, and then one backward. Frankl's ideas should be used mercifully, in small measures, as new meanings gradually emerge from the pain.

A number of writers on the Holocaust have expressed opinions which deviate from those of Frankl. Primo Levi agrees with Frankl that a small minority of "superior individuals, made of the stuff of martyrs and saints", managed to remain true to their moral codes in the camp (Levi n.d.: 98). But the general trend among the inmates that Levi describes, is a far cry from the search for meaning on which Frankl focuses. Levi noticed that survival became of prime concern in the camp, and moral convictions faded away:

> There comes to light the existence of two particularly well differentiated categories of men—the saved and the drowned. Other pairs of opposites (the good and the bad, the wise and the foolish, the cowards and the courageous, the unlucky and the fortunate) are considerably less distinct, they seem less essential, and above all they allow for more numerous and complex intermediary gradations … Here the struggle to survive is without respite, because everyone is desperately and ferociously alone. (Levi n.d.: 93–94)

In a moving chapter, titled "The last one", Levi describes the death of one of the inmates who dared to resist the authorities—he was "the last one". The camp authorities have turned the other humans, who had been capable of moral choices and judgements, into machines incapable of using their will, automatically doing what their masters want. At the end of the chapter Levi concludes:

> To destroy a man is difficult, almost as difficult as to create one: it has not been easy, nor quick, but you Germans have succeeded. Here we are, docile under your gaze; from our side you have nothing more to fear; no acts of violence, no words of defiance, not even a look of judgement. (156)

After the departure of the German soldiers, the humanity of the prisoners resurges when they decide to reward three well-deserving men among them with extra slices of bread.

> Only a day before a similar event would have been inconceivable. The law of the Lager said: 'eat your own bread, and if you can, that of your neighbour', and left no room for gratitude. It really meant that the Lager was dead … It was the first human gesture that occurred among us. I believe that that moment can be dated as the beginning of the change by which we who had not died, slowly changed from Häftlinge [prisoners] to men again. (Levi n.d.: 166)

Levi's sharp observations remind us that ethical behaviour is not merely an individual matter. Cruel authorities can create an environment where it becomes increasingly difficult, almost impossible, to observe an ethical code. Ethics is turned upside down, and what used to be good, becomes bad, and vice versa. The most merciless, cruel soldier is then the "best" one; the most servile subject of an unjust authority does "best". Consciences disappear, and human beings change into animals, or machines.

When Levi returns from the camp, he has a recurring dream:

> A dream full of horror has still not ceased to visit me, at sometimes frequent, sometimes longer, intervals … It is a dream within a dream, varied in detail, one in substance. I am sitting at a table with my family, or with friends, or at work, or in the green countryside; in short, in a peaceful yet relaxed environment,

> apparently without tension or affliction; yet I feel a deep and subtle anguish, the definite sensation of an impending threat. And in fact, as the dream proceeds, slowly or brutally, each time in a different way, everything collapses and disintegrates around me, the scenery, the walls, the people, while the anguish becomes more intense and more precise. Now everything has changed to chaos; I am alone in the centre of a grey and turbid nothing, and now I *know* what this thing means, and I also know that I have always known it; I am in the Lager once more, and nothing is true outside the Lager. All the rest was a brief pause, a deception of the senses, a dream; my family, nature in flower, my home. Now this inner dream, this dream of peace, is over, and in the outer dream which continues, gelid, a well-known voice resounds: a single word, not imperious, but brief and subdued. It is the dawn command of Auschwitz, a foreign word, feared and expected: get up, "*Wstawách*". (379–380)

Levi's narratives about life in Auschwitz complements Frankl's *logotherapy*—he reminds us that the search for meaning is not merely a personal matter, but one that involves the building of a society that allows and encourages ethical behaviour. Levi's dream suggests that humans can create either a secure and fair society or an environment where the mighty rule without morality—Levi has experienced both. The choice is ours and, echoing Frankl once more, we can indeed say:

> "Since Auschwitz we know what man is capable of. And since Hiroshima we know what is at stake".

Reflecting on his Holocaust experience, Elie Wiesel also expresses opinions which apparently deviate from what Frankl believes. He confesses his total lack of understanding of what happened in the concentration camp, saying: "I know nothing" (Wiesel 1968:180). There is no explanation "why" such a thing happened: "Answers: I say there are none" (182). To him, "Auschwitz signifies … the defeat of the intellect that wants to find a Meaning—with a capital M—in history" (183). Therefore we must "learn to be silent" (197).

It is significant that Wiesel seems to go against his own instruction, for he breaks the silence himself. In him we find the typical inner conflict of the traumatised—he cannot understand, yet he wants to understand; he wants to remain silent about an experience that cannot be put into words, and yet he continually writes about it. In a paradoxical way, he has indeed come to some kind of an understanding of what happened—an understanding that it cannot be (completely) understood. Wiesel's criticism is not so much against those who write about their experience, but against those who write without knowing; not against those who search for some meaning in their suffering, but against those who pretend to have found the total Meaning of it, with a capital M. In his writing, he condemns those who condemn, those who pretend to understand

Auschwitz, but were not there. Wiesel knows that he understands more than they do, those judging easily from the outside—for he, unlike them, comprehends the incomprehensibility of the Holocaust.

In similar vein, Lawrence Langer writes about the "bottomless layer of incompletion" of holocaust testimonies (Langer 1993: 23). He points out that no testimony can ever contain the event in its totality; it is indeed a bottomless well. He quotes Thomas Mann's novel *Joseph and his Brothers* (*Joseph und seine Brüder*) to support his view. It is interesting, though, that in spite of Mann's acknowledgement of the limitations of human knowledge and understanding in *Joseph and his Brothers*, his great work is permeated by meaningful ideas and structures. The novel suggests that much can be discovered, even though much more remains a mystery.

A strong objection against a search for the meaning of suffering could be raised by people unwilling to ascribe any positive aspect to intense suffering. They may fear that finding meaning in suffering may imply that "suffering is OK", that we should say "yes" to life in its totality, with its evil and its suffering, instead of improving the world by attempting to remove evil and suffering from it. Instead of saying "yes" to suffering, they would much rather say "no" to it. Those who have personally experienced the intense horror of trauma are not inclined to accept it placidly and regard it as a way of enriching their lives.

One should, however, distinguish between the causes and the effects of suffering. In the realisation that traumas can destroy people, physically and mentally, we should fight to remove, as far as possible, the causes of trauma: hunger, war, criminality, poverty, Aids, rape, and so on. But, in the realisation that suffering will always be with us, we should also work at softening the effects of trauma. Finding words to express pain and finding meaning in suffering (the themes of this chapter) are ways of healing their painful wounds. We do not maintain that suffering is all right—on the contrary, because it is so terrible, it is essential to gain some meaning from it to counterbalance the losses it causes. Being happy about one's own suffering is masochism; being happy about the suffering of others is sadism; it is not our intention to propagate either masochism or sadism, but to suggest ways to make suffering more bearable. The reality of trauma's destructive power can be balanced by the reality of human resilience, triumphing over adversity and creating meaning in the void.

African responses to suffering

Our argument is that one should not attempt to shut out all pain from one's life. It is a natural tendency, very marked in the modern Western world, to ignore suffering. Susan Sontag detects a

> modern sensibility, which regards suffering as something that is a mistake or an accident or a crime. Something to be fixed. Something to be refused. Something that makes one feel powerless. (Sontag 2004: 88)

On the other hand she also believes that it is

> a good in itself to acknowledge, to have enlarged, one's sense of how much suffering caused by human wickedness there is in the world we share with others. Someone who is perennially surprised that depravity exists, who continues to feel disillusioned (even incredulous) when confronted with evidence of what humans are capable of inflicting in the way of gruesome, hands-on cruelties upon other humans, has not reached moral or psychological adulthood.
>
> No one after a certain age has the right to this kind of innocence, or superficiality, to this degree of ignorance, or amnesia. (Sontag 2004: 102)

In a way that seems foreign to the modern Western mind, suffering is central to the African experience. The point is made by the character Blanche, administrator of a hospital in Zululand in J M Coetzee's *Elizabeth Costello*. Referring to the harsh life of Africa, she says:

> This is reality: the reality of Zululand, the reality of Africa. It is the reality now and the reality of the future as far as we can see it. Which is why African people come to church to kneel before Jesus on the cross, African women above all, who have to bear the brunt of reality. Because they suffer and he suffers with them. (Coetzee 2003: 141)

The African scholar Gabriel Setiloane makes a similar point: "to Africans, the crucified Jesus is irresistible" (Setiloane, quoted in Brand 2002: 67).

Gerrit Brand extensively discusses the debates around suffering and sacrifices in African Christian theology (2002: 147–194). "Sacrifice is one of the most widely discussed topics in African Christian theology," he maintains (147). Mercy Oduyoye, basing her theology on her experience as an African woman, points to the various ways in which ordinary people are senselessly sacrificed daily to the mighty and the rich. In contrast to this evil suffering, Oduyoye notes another kind of suffering, a praiseworthy suffering for the sake of others:

> "Living for others" might take the form of "dying for friends". In times of a crisis a sacrifice must be offered if the harmony and wholeness of life is to be restored … In Oduyoye's view … the Western (and Western feminist) ideal of maximal individual self-fulfilment, constrained only by the self-fulfilment of other individuals, is simply not a live option for African women and children … In a situation where people depend on one another for their very survival, "wholeness of life" will have to take the form of communal wholeness. This means that

> individual self-fulfilment can only be found in sacrificing one's personal interest for the community, and self-confidence only gained through self-denial. (Brand 2002: 163–164).

Oduyoye's ideas are echoed by the African theologian Manas Buthelezi, who distinguishes between "oppressive" and "redemptive" suffering. "Oppressive suffering" should be resisted; resistance against such oppression, however, involves the risk of another kind of suffering, redemptive suffering (Brand 2002: 166–167).

Oduyoye's and Buthelezi's opinions on suffering and sacrifice are closely linked to *ubuntu*, the much-discussed, many-faceted ethical concept developed in Africa. The following exposition is based on P H Coetzee & A P J Roux's book, *Philosophy from Africa* (pages 41 to 51). At the heart of *ubuntu* is the belief that "a person is a person through other people". *Ubuntu* is a humaneness that radiates into every aspect of life and finds its expression in a community where the individual lives for the community, and the community cares for the individual. It takes seriously the view that humans are social beings; it implies an obligation of the privileged towards the needy.

Ubuntu steers midway between the two extremes of individualism and collectivism. In contrast to individualism's belief that "self-preservation is the first law of life", it affirms that

> we cannot preserve self without being concerned about preserving other selves … The agony of the poor impoverishes the rich; the betterment of the poor enriches the rich. The manager's success at managing depends on the co-operation of the managed … Whatever affects one directly, affects all indirectly. (R Khoza, quoted in Coetzee & Roux 1998: 45)

Unlike collectivism with its disregard for the individual,

> *ubuntu* would seem to be broadening respect for the individual—respect for the individual and the rights of each person in the social unit—and purging collectivism of its negative elements. (Coetzee & Roux 1998: 45)

Although the concept is embedded in the African family and African kinship, it has been expanded to include the belief in a universal brother- and sisterhood. According to Khoza, *ubuntu* can never be racist, for it is based on respect for all human beings. The important point for the argument here is that *ubuntu* entails, on the one hand, a society of harmony and wholeness but, on the other hand, a willingness of individuals to suffer for the well-being of others.

Patterns of death and life

There is another kind of positive suffering, not specifically included in *ubuntu*; it is not so much directly linked to the needs of the community as to the growth of a person. "Is becoming always filled with pain?" (*Is alle wording pyn?*) asks the Afrikaans poet N P van Wyk Louw in one of his sonnets, and the rest of the poem suggests that growth (becoming) and pain are indeed inextricably linked, for growth often involves taking leave of cherished patterns and familiar securities. Just as biological life is characterised by the continuous formation of new cells and the dying of old ones ("death-life patterns"), a healthy inner life is characterised by continual letting go of the old and acceptance of the new; in contrast, the rejection of painful but necessary change leads to spiritual rigor mortis. This argument in favour of change seems to refute our previous argument in favour of continuity in life narratives—yet a good life narrative is characterised by constancy amidst change. Continuity is attained through ethical values that pervade the whole narrative—ethical values that are constant yet supple; remaining true to themselves, they can adapt to changing circumstances.

In a well-structured literary narrative, there is coherence between the story and its ending; the end in a way contains the whole preceding narrative. Similarly, in human life, the end is foreshadowed by what precedes it. A great trauma with its destruction is like a premonition of death. Trauma, however, can give rise to new meaning, just as a human life can continue, even after death, to spread its significance, as was discussed above with reference to Leopold's poem "Oinou hena stalagmon". Furthermore, people who are willing to suffer the "pain of becoming" and of "redemptive suffering", extend the death-life patterns mentioned above into their lives, like ripples from the great waves of trauma and death, creating coherence through the recurrence of a pattern. The death-life pattern transforms, in the formulation of Frank Kermode, the *chronos* of our moments into *kairos,* where *chronos* refers to passing moments that disappear, and *kairos* to "a point in time filled with significance, charged with a meaning derived from its relation to the end" (Kermode 1967: 47). The life narrative with *kairoi* consists of meaningful moments where new life continually emerges from the painful severing of the old; where every part has a place in a pattern characteristic of the whole.

An example of this death-life pattern is found in *Disgrace*, the novel by J M Coetzee which is analysed in chapter 5. The main character, Lucy, embodiment in the text of ethical ideals, has to go through two traumas: an "outer" and an "inner" one. Firstly, she is raped by three men, which temporarily drains the life from her; and after that she has to go through a complete inner renewal—she has "to start at ground level" (Coetzee 1999: 205), letting go of her previous wishes and perceptions in order to ensure a place for her on the farm where she wants to be. Through this death of the old, she receives a new lease of life; she reaches peace and inner freedom, because she has become willing to be the person that she feels she should be. The second crisis is maybe just as painful as the first.

The fact that, in well-structured literary narratives and in human lives, we can find coherence between the end and the preceding events does not mean that literary narratives or human lives are like boxes of chocolates, with a clearly defined form and a sweet content. On the contrary: sophisticated novels mostly have “open ends”, suggestions that various future possibilities exist, and that readers may never attach one final meaning to a story; similarly, it is impossible to interpret a human life finally when it has come to an end. Final closure evades us in the “reading” of human lives as well as in literary narratives.

Living the best of possible lives, creating a value-filled narrative from our lives, we have argued, necessarily entails pain—the pain linked to personal growth, the pain of being conscious of others’ suffering, and the pain of sacrifice for the sake of the needy in the community. For the healing of individuals and societies, it is necessary to fight against “oppressive suffering”, but to accept “redemptive suffering”.

Paradoxical answers

The answers to our most profound questions often lie in paradoxes which can contain the contrasts and contradictions of life. We should fight pain, yet realise it is inherent in human existence; remove suffering as far as possible, yet face it as part of life; we should acknowledge the terror of trauma, yet try to transform it into something meaningful, thus balancing the loss with gain. Those labouring for the healing of society, are themselves “wounded healers”, to borrow a phrase from Henri Nouwen (1972); hurt by their own pain and the pain of the world, yet with an inner wholeness, willing to do what should be done. In a society that is deeply divided, like the South African one, with its on-going conflicts, complete harmony is unattainable, yet we must work towards total reconciliation as if it were attainable, for without such an effort society will fall apart.

We should transform our lives into the best of possible narratives. We have to admit to ourselves that some of the gaps in our life narratives will never be closed, certain things will never be understood, and total closure and coherence is unattainable. And yet we have to search for the maximum of meaningful patterns—we must fill our existence with values that endure, even in times of agony and despair. We should resist the desire to make superficial romantic comedies from our lives, and strive rather for a narrative containing the fullness of life, with its joys and its sorrows, reflecting a tragic optimism.

CHAPTER TWO

UNACKNOWLEDGED TRAUMA: BETWEEN SILENCE AND DISCLOSURE

As we enter the new millennium, it is disheartening to note that wars, genocide, and crimes against humanity have not subsided since the atrocities of World War II that inspired the cry: *Never Again.* Human misery that has resulted from gross human rights abuses across the globe is on the rise, and its extent has been made visible by the increasing number of people internally displaced within their own countries, and those forced into exile, fleeing wars and torture in their homelands. A survey conducted by the United States Committee for Refugees in 2000 estimated the number of refugees and asylum seekers world-wide to be approximately 14 million. The effects of trauma on individuals and communities—particularly human-induced trauma such as mass political violence—can be profound. Many of the people fleeing from extreme conditions of violence and abuse in their home countries bear indelible psychological scars of the traumas they experienced there.

Extreme experiences of trauma are overwhelming. They can be understood as experiences that threaten one's sense of emotional, physical, and social integrity. The overwhelming effect of trauma ruptures the multiple layers of the ego's protective organisational fabric. This organising matrix of the ego includes a number of aspects: the individual's basic assumptions about the world, such as belief system and sense of trust in others, physical aspects of one's body, social networks, and so on. The rupture of the organisational matrix has implications for the way the traumatic circumstances are remembered.

Early conceptualisation of trauma by Freud and Breuer (Breuer & Freud 1936) point out that traumatic affect, that is to say traumatic reaction to traumatic experience, is determined by "whether there has been an energetic reaction to the event that provokes [the traumatic] affect" (1936: 8). Thus, as Judith Herman (1992) has pointed out, when traumatic experience induces helplessness and powerlessness, the traumatic situation takes away the individual's ability to react and to take any action. Taking this further, it might be said that traumatic events that produce traumatic effects create a void. This state of absence is the condition that, in part, leads to the rupture and the shattering of the self: what Susan Brison (1995) has termed "unmaking". This notion of the "unmaking" of the self is similar to early psychoanalytic formulations by Charcot, Janet, Breuer, and Freud, who argued that extreme forms of trauma lead to some kind of psychic rupture, a tearing apart of the integrity of the self. This rupture of psychic integrity affects the way that traumatic memories are encoded. Memories of trauma are not encoded in the same way as normal experiences. They are stored in dissociated and fragmented form, and often dominate the mental life of victims of trauma (Van der Kolk, 1989; Beveridge, 1998). Yet even as traumatic memories intrude into the lives of trauma victims, there is a struggle, simultaneously, to avoid the images of traumatic experience. Reisner (2002) argues that the pressure to avoid trauma "is the single most pervasive individual and cultural response to traumatic circumstances" (13).

This tension between intrusive memory and avoidance of trauma renders the traumatic memory difficult to assimilate. There is scholarly evidence that shows how traumatic memories, and difficulties in their assimilation, often return as behavioural re-enactment, both at the interpersonal level and within societies. The phenomenon of re-enactment and its centrality in the lives of people who have been exposed to life-threatening experiences of trauma is well established in traumatic stress research (Kernberg 2003, Laub & Lee 2003). These re-enactments manifest in acts of revenge, anger, and sometimes as violence against the self, and may seem unrelated and disconnected from the original trauma.

One might say therefore that re-enactments such as acts of revenge are symbolic acts or reactions, and suggest an attempt to fill the void created by the helplessness and powerlessness induced by the trauma. They continue to affect people who have suffered trauma, in part because the traumatic experience has not been fully integrated into the individual's psychic and cognitive schemas, and instead exists in fragmented and dissociated form.

The goal of intervention in the lives of people who have been traumatised is to help them integrate traumatic memory in order to *transform* the force of the traumatic memory into something positive. Language offers the possibility of the transformation of trauma into narrative. The significance of narrative lies not simply in remembering trauma, but in its transformation through language.

A state of being frozen

All traumatic narrative and description of traumatic events, Kyo Maclear observes, constitute "limits of remembrance" because the horrors being recounted "conjure an excess that cannot be retold" (1999: 235). Extreme trauma is "unspeakable" precisely because of the inadequacy of language to fully convey victims' experiences. This is part of the reason why trauma survivors struggle with transforming their experiences into narrative. Many survivors of atrocities such as the Holocaust have commented on this tension between traumatic events they lived through and the language available to describe them. Primo Levi, survivor of the Nazi concentration camps, has expressed it thus: "our language lacks words to express this offence" (Levi 1985: 9)[1]. Yet despite its limitations, speech is necessary, not only to re-capture the traumatic event, but also to restore the victim's sense of self and to help him or her regain control over a self shattered by the trauma. Reconstructing the trauma into narrative form is one of the most crucial processes in the journey towards the victim's healing. "Bearing witness", as trauma scholars have termed the process of telling one's story of trauma, is an important part of "working through" trauma.

When people are overwhelmed by a traumatic experience, there is a silencing of the senses, a state of being frozen. The silencing is more than a lack of words; it is also a lack of understanding of what has happened to them. Trauma overwhelms the psyche; it contains no reference point in terms of one's former experience. The word "frozen" comes up many times in the story of women who have been raped, because they do not know how to deal with the experience; they do not have the resources to deal with it or the capacity to respond to it. It is an experience which they have gone through but which they cannot comprehend because it has not been articulated; they do not have the language to tell what they have experienced, and therefore they cannot understand. When people say, "I cannot explain it", and we as observers say, "It is unspeakable", it means precisely that: it is something for which we cannot find language because it is so overwhelming, so unreal, as if it had not happened. You cannot believe it, even as it is happening to you.

It is this "unbelievability" that makes trauma so difficult to articulate, to find words for. What is stilled, what is frozen, is understanding, the language to express it, and the emotions to feel it. When we remember the trauma, we remember it in fragments, in dissociated bits, and we have to piece these fragments together. Part of the struggle of healing from trauma is the struggle to find the appropriate language to narrate the trauma.

Under normal circumstances we know who we are and we know what capacity we have to respond to experiences, but when trauma overwhelms us,

---

[1] Paul Fussel, however, suggests that the challenge is less with language than what listeners want to hear. The English language, he argues, is rich in words and phrases that can adequately describe the horrors of atrocities. The problem, he states, "[is] less one of 'language' than of gentility and optimism [of listeners] .... What listener wants to be torn and shaken when he doesn't have to be? We have made unspeakable mean indescribable...." (Fussel 1975: 170).

we lose the capacity to engage and to interact. Trauma is a loss of control, a loss of understanding, a loss of identity—we wonder why we did not act in an appropriate way, a feeling of "that wasn't me". Trauma has profound after-effects: in our personal relationships and in specific situations, we respond in ways that we ourselves often do not understand. We do not realise how much our responses are affected by the unarticulated experience of trauma.

The relational aspect of narrative

The role that narrative plays in survivors' and victims' healing and recovery is well-established in the literature on trauma. Psychologists writing about trauma stress the importance of the *relational* aspect of narrative: in order for the trauma narrative to heal, one's trauma narrative has to be received by an empathic listener. Dori Laub, in his discussion of "truth, testimony, and survival" highlights the significance of others' presence as empathic listeners. "Bearing witness to a trauma," Laub observes, "is … a process that includes the listener" (1992: 70). The significance of the empathic listener for the trauma narrative is the possibility created for the victim of trauma to externalise the traumatic event.

Empathetic listening poses extraordinary challenges, as Erika Apfelbaum has pointed out:

> The only way to truly hear the survivor's narratives is to confront the world of radical otherness and to face the existential, epistemological and moral implications of its grim and frightful reality. Hearing then becomes a major challenge to our usual categories of thinking, to the logic, rationale and values on which our sociability has been constructed. It raises the question of our responsibility as citizens … In brief, true listening requires courage. (Apfelbaum 2002: 13)

When we come together to narrate our traumatic experiences, we invite others not only to listen to what we have to say, but to journey with us as we "re-find" ourselves and re-find the language that has been lost. So the journey of narrating, of being in dialogue concerning our experiences, is a very important one, because we need an audience—a person, or people, who will listen with compassion, with a desire to understand what has happened to us. The listener may be the person who caused the trauma, or someone who was present when the trauma happened, or who was not present but knows about the trauma. In the telling of the trauma, even at a stage where it cannot be articulated completely, the process provides the victims with footholds, so that in the words and gestures of those who are listening, they derive encouragement to re-find not just themselves, but also the language to talk about what has happened to them.

The collective sharing of the narratives of trauma is a critical sharing. When we come to the "table of dialogue" to share our traumas, we come with different kinds of trauma. The point is not to measure who was traumatised most, but to receive our varied experiences together so that in the listening process we are bound to each other. We create a common bond of humanity when we understand that we come to the table of dialogue with different kinds of trauma, all of which are important. The challenge is, how do we listen to each other and how do we navigate the path of telling our stories, so that we can hear, not only hear as in the organic process of hearing, but hear deeply, from a profound place, what each is saying to the others; to understand that we come from different paths, bringing our traumas and wanting to connect with one another through our stories. The challenge is to be bound by human sharing, by human moments that connect us as human beings who have been hurt in different ways. That is the importance of story-telling: to bring us together and to connect us, to allow us to listen to what the others are saying and not to judge, but to listen to the sound of pain in each of our hearts.

The remaking of the self

Susan Brison (2002) elaborates on the idea of narrative as a "remaking" of the self. Trauma, she argues, robs the self of its sense of autonomy and leads to loss of control of oneself—what she terms the "undoing" of the self. The act of transforming trauma into narrative, Brison informs us, and others' ability and willingness to listen empathetically "enables survivors to gain more control over the traces left by the trauma" (2002: 71). This entails regaining control over a previously shattered self; a process of "remaking" the self. Narrating traumatic memory therefore can be understood as a piecing together of a "dismembered self", an attempt at re-mastering traumatic memory. According to Brison, this involves:

> [a] shift from being the object or medium of someone else's (the perpetrator's) speech … to being the subject of one's own. The act of bearing witness to the trauma facilitates this shift, not only by transforming traumatic memory into a narrative that can be worked into the survivor's sense of self … but also by reintegrating the survivor into a community, re-establishing connections essential to selfhood. (2002: 68)

Carmella B'hahn (2002) agrees with Brison. Through telling and listening, "giving and receiving our life experiences" B'hahn writes, "we weave the human tapestry into a sense of community" which accelerates transformation of the self and "prevents the numbing pain of separation" (2002: 18).

The acknowledgement of trauma is well-established in psychoanalytic literature as an important vehicle for helping victims of trauma regain their sense of self in relation to others. Nicholas Rand (1994), writing in the introduction to *The Shell and the Kernel* by Nicolas Abraham and Maria Torok captures the issue of the recognition of one's trauma as follows:

> Explicit acknowledgement of the full extent and ramifications of the patient's suffering is one of the analyst's crucial functions. Whether with our own strength, with the help of loved ones, or with an analyst if need be, we must be able to remember the past, recall what was taken from us, understand and grieve over what we have lost to trauma, *and so find and renew ourselves* (Abraham & Turok 1994: 12–13, italics added).

This understanding of the role of narrating trauma and its centrality in the "reconstruction" of the self raises an important question: what happens when the audience, individual or collective, is not willing to engage as empathic listener to the survivor's trauma narrative? What is the form through which trauma can be told and listened to when the traumatic events are being denied by the listener? How can victims bear witness to events that no one wants to hear about? The notion of "unspeakable" in such cases is not simply a question of language limitations. The problem is that of unspeakable trauma vexed by hardened silence and secrecy: a trauma that has become "a secret that will not be revealed" (Moreiras 1996: 204). If, as Judith Herman suggests, the only thing that can help integrate traumatic experience and heal trauma is "the use of words" (Herman 1992: 183), how can the effects of trauma be transcended if its memory is banished to unacknowledged silence?

Between silence and disclosure

It is to the question of unacknowledged and unexpressed trauma that we now wish to turn. If narrating one's trauma is important for its integration into one's sense of being and one's recovery from its debilitating effects, what happens when victims' suffering is not recognised by others, when victims are silenced?

Early writings on trauma have speculated that the overwhelming nature of trauma renders it mentally and emotionally inaccessible to its victims. This insight has endured, and continues to be central in current conceptualisation of trauma.

The process of telling is daunting, even terrifying; it forces one to focus on one's feelings, but they are exactly what is unknown. When we are traumatised, we are not clear about our feelings, because they have in many cases been disassociated, split off, from the reality of the traumatic experience, and we talk around the trauma because it is so frightening. In the midst of talking about a trauma people will often say, "You cannot imagine", and they break down crying. They break down crying because tears can take the place of words—the language of tears, the body language. Although the tears are an expression, they are not in the language of words—the fear of the unknown trauma remains. People who have suffered trauma have to confront the trauma, and their feelings around the trauma, but when that moment of potential confrontation comes, everything comes to a standstill.

When one invites a victim to revisit the trauma, one is saying, "Face it; here is that feeling that you ran away from. You have to confront it for your survival." Yet, paradoxically, it is also for their survival that the victims of trauma do not want to face the trauma. They are afraid, they do not want to open up, but at the same time they know that to begin the journey towards healing they need to find the words to navigate the trauma. Indeed, the process of healing trauma is directly linked to the process of finding language to narrate it. It is about telling the story so that it becomes part of one's identity and part of one's life narrative, so that it is told in the same way that we talk about ordinary events—so that one does not have to stop to say, "You cannot imagine", so that one says, by implication, "You *can* actually imagine it, because it happened to me and this is how it happened."

Scholars agree that the psychic imprints of trauma "cry out" for articulation even if they are not fully grasped, or indeed known, by those who experience them. What seems to be suggested by this is that "trauma will out" in one way or another, in spite of being silenced or denied. Cathy Caruth (1995) addresses the issue of the inevitability of this "outing" of trauma in her book *Unclaimed Experience.* Trauma, she argues, is bound to return to haunt the survivor; it "imposes itself" repeatedly in the nightmares and repetitive actions of the survivor. Trauma is "always a story of a wound that cries out" (Caruth 1995: 4).

The following South African story illustrates the ambivalence in the way in which victims and survivors sometimes approach the past: a strong pull towards forgetting, or rather a denial of memory, while at the same time there is a deep need to recall the details of the trauma.

A woman whose eleven year-old son had been killed by the police in the township of Mlungisi in Queenstown in 1986 confronted me when I (P G-M) was working for the Truth and Reconciliation Commission (TRC): "Why did you come here? Why did you come here?" I followed her outside, where she began to cry, and continued to speak through her uncontrollable sobbing: "Have you come here to hurt us? Just tell me, have you come here to open our scars?" She continued to speak with a mixture of tears and anger and said that the TRC was "a pointless exercise", she had forgotten her pain and had "put grass over the past", using a Xhosa expression. "And now you want us to remember? Is this going to bring back my son?" the woman said tearfully.

I later accompanied her to her home, where she invited me in. She pointed me to a chair and sat in another one facing the only window in the room, her eyes contemplative but also sorrowful as the afternoon sun shone on her face. Then remarkably, she started to tell her story:

"My son was eleven. He came home during school break at ten o'clock. I was sitting right there where you are sitting, just sitting exactly where you are sitting in that chair. He walked in dressed in his school uniform and went to the cupboard over there and cut himself a slice of bread. He is doing all of this in a rush. He is like that when he comes home during break. He spread peanut butter on it and then put the rest of the bread back, leaving the crumbs all over the cupboard, and the knife, still smudged with peanut butter. He ran out. He is still chewing his bread and holding it in his hand. It wasn't long—I heard shots outside. Some commotion and shouts. Then I'm hearing, "*uThemba, uThemba, nank'uThemba bamdubule*!" (It's Themba, they've shot Themba!) and then someone calling out for me: "*Mama kaThemba!*" (Themba's mother!). I went flying out of this house. Now I am dazed. I ran, not thinking. My eyes are on the crowd that has gathered. Here is my son, my only child. It was just blood all over. My anguish was beyond anything I ever thought I could experience. They have finished him. I threw myself over. I can feel the wetness of his blood—I felt his last breath leave him. He was my only child."

Her "exploded silence" is a narrative that speaks of the world where helpless parents grieved because they could not protect their children inside or outside the home, but could only cover over the memory of their grief and hope that, someday, grass would grow over it. For one brief moment on a sunny afternoon, she had brushed the silence aside, pushed the grass back to let me see her deepest memory and the shards of pain that lay beneath. The pieces of that fateful day were still shattered, like broken china that cannot be put back together. The "indelible images" of her traumatised memory—the crumbs on the cupboard, the knife, still smudged with peanut butter, the chair positioned exactly there—all these items had in her mind become symbols of her little Themba's final act at home, the last things he touched that are not covered in blood, that can be recovered as symbols of an orderly daily life. Even the image of the crumbs is treasured as some kind of a sacred memory. Her memory of the fateful day is recalled and represented by broken pieces, symbolising the broken body of her son and her own broken dreams for his life. In a sense, the cupboard, the bread, the peanut butter, the knife are all crumbs, pieces that no longer fit together into a coherent whole or life story. But these crumbs and pieces are recalled because they are the only things in her memory of that day that are not spattered in blood—to be buried under the grass.

Judith Herman (1992) explains how victims of trauma struggle at one and the same time with silence and with disclosure of trauma. She refers to the "dialectic of trauma", the tension between remembering and forgetting traumatic experience. Victims want to forget because remembering reopens the wound of trauma; at the same time, they want to remember because silence is unbearable. To remember, to narrate trauma, even individual trauma, means to honour one's own memory. It also honours silenced voices from the past, and beckons us to a future where we will no longer be silent.

Narrating individual and collective trauma is essential for describing the past. Traumatic narrative penetrates to the deepest levels of the human spirit and invites the empathy that characterises our essential humanity. Susan Brison observes that silencing, by others, of trauma narratives comes not only from an absence of empathy with victims, but also out of an active fear of empathising with those whose terrifying fate forces us to acknowledge that we are not in control of our own … As a society, we live with the unbearable by pressuring those who have been traumatised to forget and by rejecting the testimonies of those who are forced by fate to remember (Brison 2002: 57).

The necklace game

I now wish to illustrate, through another story, the idea of trauma's return to "impose" itself on the lives of victims. It is an incident that involved a group of young girls from a township in the Eastern Cape. The story is an example of the way in which unacknowledged trauma is often passed on from one generation to the next, from victims to their descendants, and of the uncanny way in which trauma, in spite of its silencing, is repeated and "acted out".

"Let's play a game." It was strange, almost surreal, to see a group of young girls, seven to ten years old, laughing and cavorting in the streets of Mlungisi Township—a township that in the mid-1980s had been the scene of so much misery, a tinderbox of inflamed emotion against the inhumanities of apartheid; but that was before these children had even been born.

I was doing some work in Mlungisi and happened to be walking through their neighbourhood when I saw them. Their squeals and cries were the very embodiment of joy. My heart leapt. They looked like little tender shoots of foliage, little blades of life, poking out from under the cooled lava of a township once utterly devastated by apartheid's volcano.

"What game?" the others shouted, skipping back and forth.

"Let me show you," the first one said. She was about eight and looked as if she might be the informal leader of the group. She began to demonstrate. The other girls did not seem too enthusiastic about this new game. What was wrong with just playing skip? But slowly, they became intrigued.

"It's called the necklace game," the leader said. "This is just going to be pretend necklace, not the real thing," she said. She pushed the other girls aside as if to open up the stage. Rotating through the role of victim, then killers, then onlookers, she seemed to my amazement to recall virtually everything that actually happened in a real "necklace" murder, even though she had not been born when the last necklace killing occurred in her township.

She flailed her arms, screaming in mock anguish as if being beaten, swaying back and forth, turning her head from left to right and begging for mercy with eyes wide open to show fright. Then she switched roles and play-acted someone going off to find gasoline, then another person offering matches, then someone running to demand a car tyre from an imaginary passing motorist.

"Give me your tyre!" she ordered with mock hostility. She narrated the part of the motorist dutifully obeying, then the gasoline man, then the matches man. Finally, she returned to her victim role, struggling against the make-believe tyre being placed around the neck. Nervously, she made a gesture simulating the striking of a match, as if her friends—now a crowd of executors—had forced her to light herself up.

As imaginary flames engulfed her, she threw her arms wildly into the air. "Now sing and dance and clap your hands. I'm dying," she said. Her friends started clapping and singing in a discordant rhythm. They formed a circle and went round and round her "body". Gradually, the high-pitched screams of the girl with the imaginary tyre around her neck faded into a whimper as her life "ebbed away". "Consumed" by the flames, she slowly lowered herself to the ground and "died". It was all make-believe.

None of the girls I saw that morning re-enacting the necklacing had actually seen a necklace murder. But the unspoken events of the past—the silence of Mlungisi's lambs—had become imprinted on their minds. It was not just the outward form of the game, but its inner meaning, the sense of trauma to communal life that it carried with it. They carried the collective fear and horror somewhere deep within them. Re-enacting the death dance of a necklace victim may well have been a way of transforming its memory into something more accessible, and less fearful for the girls.

This incident provides an illuminating metaphor for the way in which trauma is passed on intergenerationally "in ways subtle and not so subtle",[2] through silences, through fear, and through the psychological scars and pain that are often left unacknowledged. The "language" of trauma is etched in the memory of many victims of traumatic experience and passed on to the next generation, and to the next, in the way that traumatic memory so often does.

Trauma will out. Trauma will out, despite being silenced, because it demands psychic assimilation. Attempts to wipe trauma from history—to efface

[2] Laub & Lee: *Thanatos and Massive Psychic Trauma.*

it—through denial and silencing will not prevent the disclosure that cries out for expression. This disclosure can happen in symbolic form, or in actual narrative form. The group of young girls playing the "necklace game" may not be aware of the links between their "dance" and their community's trauma. Even to the young girl who is the leader of the group the "memory" of the trauma may be unknown. "Not knowing" trauma is not only relevant here because the young girls did not experience it directly. The issue of the chasm between knowing and not-knowing trauma is the foundation of Cathy Caruth's book, *Unclaimed Experience*. She uses the metaphor of a "double wound" to address the question of trauma re-enactment as the second wounding, one that occurs after the trauma, which is the first wound. According to Caruth, it is an irony that trauma is identifiable only "in the way in which its very unassimilated nature—the way it was precisely *not known* in the first instance—returns to haunt the survivor later on" (Caruth 1995: 4). Elie Wiesel also speaks about the chasm between trauma and how it is remembered:

> Ask any survivor; he will tell you, he who has not lived the event will never know it. And he who went through it will not reveal it, not really, not entirely. Between his memory and his reflection there is a wall—and it cannot be pierced. (1997: 405)

The externalised parodying of a necklace murder could be seen as an expression of that which is as-yet-unknown, "unclaimed" experience, to use Caruth's metaphor. It is the unavoidable disclosure of the trauma through the young girls' "death dance" that makes known the trauma and history of the "necklace". The death game, in fact, *speaks* of the loss suffered through necklace murders, yet it also transcends knowledge of its massive trauma. For how can we fathom the enormity of a trauma if its telling begins with the words: "Let's play a game"?

As with the game that the young girls play, when traumatic events from the past "reappear" in the lives of victims—whether direct victims of the trauma or their descendants—it seems that the repetition of trauma not only externalises it, but also transforms it into ritual, making it more assailable. It is perhaps a cathartic way of putting into action the struggle to find language to express the frustrations, helplessness, and disempowerment associated with the original trauma. The story of the necklace "dance" was a poignant one, shocking, yet remarkable in the way in which the young enactors of their community's collective trauma created fiction, perhaps without knowing it, out of pain. The allegorical juxtaposition of the necklace memory with its dramatic enactment casts the girls as fictional characters, or as reincarnated lives of those unnamed and unnameable dead who were lost through the brutality of the necklace murders. Through their theatrical narration, the girls are testimony to and living proof of the traumas suffered by their community, traumas that refuse to be silenced. Words from T S Eliot come to mind: "These fragments I have shored against my ruins."[3] The image is of a broken person trying helplessly, not altogether with success, to recover some sense of coherence in an inner world that has become broken, a world where the ever-present trauma refuses to be silenced.

Re-enactments of trauma

The story of the past continues to be unfinished as long as it is not spoken about. Those girls were enacting the necklace in a skit, a play in the streets. What are the other forms through which the necklace is going to be enacted by these same girls in their adult life? The children of the necklace game were not present during any necklacing. When I encountered them, the necklacings had happened ten years before. They had never witnessed a necklacing, yet it was clear to me that they had picked up the history. One of them, perhaps the leader of the group, must have lost a loved one, and would have heard the story told in their family—and they were now repeating the story. Re-enactment of trauma happens in many forms, one of the most dangerous of which is the repetition of violence.

When people are traumatised, it is an experience of humiliation; they are powerless and they need a sense of control; the violation takes away the very core of who you are. When people repeat these traumas, it is as an effort to be in a place where they are in control once more; it is the reclaiming of their power and the sense of control that was taken away from them by the perpetrators. They put themselves in the shoes of the perpetrator, thereby becoming perpetrators themselves. This little play by the children was a skit, but it is a chilling one because it speaks of the presence of memories, memories which are still bubbling there. Who knows what will happen when these children become adults?

Re-enactments of trauma happen in many countries that have had endlessly repeated conflict. It is not only important that one should talk about past traumas: how one talks about them is equally important. We hear people talking about conflicts as if they were happening in the here and now, whereas they are conflicts linked to generations gone before. In Bosnia, former Yugoslavia, present conflicts are traced to six centuries ago; in Rwanda the same thing happens. In America many African Americans talk about the times of slavery and they link that to the slavery that they say continues today. How often do we hear people talking about conflict and are not able to figure out whether it is

---

[3] *The Waste Land*, line 430.

something that happened last week or last year or ten years ago or centuries ago?

Repetition of trauma takes place because there is something unfinished. Dialogue with one another across different groups is vital, and in this dialogue we should not only remember past traumas, but work through them and transcend them, making sure that we understand that what happened belongs to the past. No more should we say: "My forefathers fought against your forefathers in the battle of such and such, that's why the anger is still there."

The dialogue of narratives should bring us together so that we understand clearly that we are a new people, breaking with the past, committed to a different life, to forging new and different relationships with one another. We should not be people frozen in the past; we should be moving forward. That is the importance of the narratives of our traumas—that they should help us find a way of remembering that does not increase the divide but brings us together. That is the challenge that is always before us.

Sometimes people belonging to the group of the oppressors do not want to apologise because to them an apology is an admission of guilt. Hearing that they are guilty and that they benefited from the past, threatens their sense of self-respect. So their denial is an attempt to protect themselves from feeling as evil as those who perpetrated evil in their name. I think the burden is on victims to transcend their victim role, to find the generosity and grace to suspend their accusatory feelings. By setting aside their accusatory attitude, they allow perpetrators to forget—at least temporarily—that they are perpetrators or that they are associated with perpetrators, and this allows them to reach into the depths of their humanness. The victims allow the perpetrators to refocus on their humanness, on their shared humanity, and that is when perpetrators are able to reflect humanly on their deeds or on their association with certain deeds, so that they can examine their conscience. That is what enables them to say—at least—"My goodness, that was wrong; I really was associated with a terrible system." You as victim have opened the door, and you have said, "I am really coming to you as a human being and I want to embrace you as another human being," and that softens their hearts. What hardens the heart of the perpetrator is the feeling of guilt and the denial of that guilt.

Victims who approach the world with a banner of victimhood often fall into the trap of repeating the very act that was committed against them. When victims narrate their stories, the ideal is that they shed the cloak of victimhood. The sharing of narratives challenges victims to take on a new identity, that of being a survivor, of having the power to make important choices, of being able to engage with others, even others whom they are likely to identify as perpetrators.

The naming of people in our society as either victims or perpetrators can be the very thing that leads to the repetition of cycles of violence. Telling the story at a common table of dialogue challenges both victims and perpetrators to shed their old identities and discover a common humanity in sharing the compassion which forms the core of what it is to be a human being. It is critical, in these processes of narrating trauma, to re-find our identities of humanness, because that is the only way in which we will be able to hear one another. If victims continue to wear the cloak of victimhood, it closes language and dialogue; but if they shed this cloak, the door is opened for engagement with others as fellow human beings.

CHAPTER THREE

SEARCHING FOR CLOSURE: THE CRYING VOICE

Nokuthula's crying voice

Finding closure from the traumas of the past may in some instances be highly problematic. That is especially the case when the body of the deceased has not been found. In the words of Ruth Kluger:

> Where there is no grave, we are condemned to go on mourning. Or we become like animals and don't mourn at all … By a grave I don't necessarily mean a place in a cemetery, but simply clear knowledge about the death of someone you've known. (Kluger 2004: 90)

The ordinary crying of a baby reminds most mothers of the joys and challenges of motherhood. It may give them a sense of relief that for them, crying babies are a thing of the past. Some may feel pride and a sense of certainty that the children they brought up with love are today young women and men, well on the journey into adulthood. For one South African mother, Ernestina Simelane, however, the memory of the extraordinary crying of her daughter, Nokuthula, is an *event* that she cannot leave behind. Then, as now, Nokuthula's unremitting crying brought Ernestina nothing but anguish. Then, it was a source of anguished despair as Ernestina tirelessly searched for a cure for Nokuthula's relentless crying since her birth in September 1962. "I would rock her back and forth like this," Ernestina sat on a couch in her living room and gestured with her arms as if holding a baby, swinging her upper body in rocking motion, her face a reflection of the pain she felt then, "On and on like this, she would cry inconsolably, day and night. I would rock her, feed her—I tried everything, paediatricians, herbal remedies, and even traditional healers, nothing worked." And lowering her voice, as if to silence the memory, her face still a picture of the pain the memory seemed to evoke, she continued: "The crying never stopped …"

And now, Nokuthula's crying voice continues to ring through the "anguished memory" of another event that would come much later, that of Nokuthula's unsolved disappearance after she was abducted by the apartheid security police in September 1983. The trauma of Nokuthula's disappearance is a wound that has shattered Ernestina's life—a rupture in the continuity of her very being. It is a wound that refuses to heal, throbbing painfully as she tries to find words to describe her loss, and to bring order to the chaos of hope and utter hopelessness, of simultaneously knowing and not knowing the actual fate of her daughter. For more than twenty years Ernestina has knocked on doors crying for help, hoping that she will eventually get some answers. Days, weeks, months, and years of searching—all rolled into an endless spiral of traumatic memory, fragmented, orderless, and chaotic. To reclaim her sanity, Ernestina must re-order her trauma and try to make sense of it.

The essence of psychological trauma is loss: loss of language, meaning, order, and sense of continuity. Trauma is a shattering of the basic organising principles necessary to construct meaningful narratives about ourselves, others, and our environment. Early psychoanalytic formulations by Charcot, Janet, Breuer, and Freud all noted that extreme forms of trauma lead to some kind of psychic rupture and a fragmentation of traumatic memories in ways that resist integration and may dominate the mental life of many victims of trauma. Our ability to construct meaning from our experiences—to narrate memory—is fundamental to psychological health. This position was first clarified by nineteenth century psychiatrist Pierre Janet. Janet pointed out that memories about normal experiences are easily and automatically integrated into mental structures. He characterised memory as an *action*: "the action of telling a story" (Janet, quoted in Leys 2000: 111), i.e. the ability to narrate experience.

Janet argued that traumatic experience disrupts the ability to narrate the past. Elaborating on this viewpoint, Van der Kolk & Van der Hart (1995) assert that traumatic experience does not easily fit into existing cognitive schemas. Trauma resists integration into "narrative memory" and instead is "re-lived" through involuntary processes such as intrusive thoughts, nightmares, flashbacks and hallucinations. Trauma, therefore, is a disruption of the narrative-building function of the self. Accordingly, trauma recovery entails the organisation of traumatic experience into a coherent narrative about the past. "Narrating" the traumatic memory means that

> the story can be told, the person can look back at what happened; he has given it a place in his life history, his autobiography, and thereby in the whole of his personality. (van der Kolk & van der Hart 1995: 176)

Ernestina Simelane's story, which we use here to explore narrative memory in the aftermath of traumatic experience, and the many layers and forms that narrative memory takes, is drawn from interviews that I (P G-M) conducted with Ernestina when I was working as a psychologist consultant for the film *Betrayal* (Mark Kaplan, Grey Matter Media, 2006). There are striking similarities between the process of transforming trauma into narrative described in the preceding chapter, and Ernestina's attempt to piece together various themes that, for her, represent the story of her "disappeared" daughter Nokuthula.

Nokuthula Simelane, Ernestina's eldest daughter, was born in September 1962. As a young adult in the early 1980s, she was a member of the ANC (African National Congress) underground structures based in neighbouring Swaziland, and served as a courier travelling in and out of South Africa. In 1983, Nokuthula was about to complete her Bachelor of Arts degree at the University of Swaziland. There was excitement in her family about her imminent achievement. Her parents had bought her a dress and an academic gown for her graduation, and were preparing to drive to the ceremony with some of Nokuthula's siblings when they were informed that Nokuthula had not returned after a trip to South Africa. Her parents were concerned, but assumed that she would show up to receive her certificate. But there was no sign of Nokuthula on graduation day. Her parents began a search that involved travelling to many ANC centres in neighbouring countries, writing numerous letters to the Red Cross offices in these countries, speaking to high-ranking officials of the ANC, to Nokuthula's former teachers, her friends. For years Ernestina and her husband searched for their daughter. There would be stories of Nokuthula being sighted in some country, raising their hopes. Ernestina's hopes were raised again in 1990 by the unbanning of the liberation movements and the return of exiles to South Africa. In 1994, with the first democratic election, Ernestina continued to hope for news of her daughter; but she was no closer to knowing than she had been ten years earlier.

In 1997, a newspaper article appeared with a headline story about Nokuthula's disappearance.[4] A series of events that began with a confession by a former security police informant seemed to lead the Simelane family closer to the truth. Nokuthula's abduction occurred during the week of her would-be graduation when she was sent by her commander in the ANC to deliver information to South Africa. The recipient of her communiqué turned out to be a police collaborator, who laid a trap for her abduction by the Transvaal division of the security police. Subsequent to this revelation, the white and black policemen involved in Nokuthula's abduction appeared before the Truth and Reconciliation Commission (TRC). This was the family's hope of discovering the truth about their daughter. But for days they heard nothing but denials; the truth continued to elude them.

How, then does Ernestina talk about her loss, and what are the themes around which her narrative memory evolves? The challenge that Ernestina faces lies in "not knowing" her trauma—knowing her daughter has been missing for all these years, but not knowing whether she has actually *lost* her. Trauma is

---

[4] *The Sowetan*, 15 February 1995.

characterised by a loss of narrative, a loss of words. The key to psychological recovery from trauma is the assimilation of the traumatic experience into a coherently organised narrative. In other words, the loss of narrative can be reconstructed by organising the past through narrating the event. If "what happened" remains intangible and elusive, then the process of working through and healing the wounds of trauma, which can be achieved by transforming trauma into narrative, becomes a haunting and unfillable chasm of deep sorrow.

Overwhelming trauma cannot be assimilated, not only because of its overwhelming quality, but precisely because of the void created by an experience which by its very nature is inarticulable. What lies between the possibility of knowing on the one hand, and *not knowing* on the other, is a void, an unspeakable emptiness that cannot be grasped. Ernestina's problem therefore lies fundamentally in this void, in the failure of the speech act—because there *are* no words to explain what happened to Nokuthula; the facts about Nokuthula's "disappearance" remain buried in secrecy. This is the problem in which Ernestina finds herself.

In the vast landscape of this unfillable abyss, Ernestina must still find a place to "start", to reconstruct a connection with Nokuthula's *lived* life, as well as a semblance of the continuity of her own. The "one thing" she felt was threatened, she told me, was her role as mother. This is what seemed to "die" with the "disappearance" of Nokuthula; it is an identity she has had to fight to preserve.

Carmella B'hahn has remarked that the shock of overwhelming trauma brings with it "protective veils" that shield us from the brutal truth of loss. But as time passes and shock recedes, she points out, "the veils thin and blow in the wind, bringing gusts of thc physical finality of death" (2002: 33). Ernestina's trauma, it seems, does not obey this rule of time. Time does not "pass" for her, but hovers in a state of what Lawrence Langer (1991) has called "timelessness". It resists the "finality" of death, (seeing the body is the only way to confirm the certainty of death). How can there be finality when there is no body, there are no bones? The loss is made all the more traumatic because it is "unknown", it is a double trauma. To escape from it, Ernestina must confront it, face its "pastness", narrate its memory, and accept its finality. But, for her, this trauma refuses to be relegated into the past, and hence be assimilated through a coherent narrative memory that opens up the possibility of accepting finality. Instead, Ernestina narrates her trauma as if she is living *through* it, like the repetitive dramas that are typical of intrusive phenomena in trauma, such as intrusive thoughts, nightmares and flashbacks. Ernestina's narrative memory is a mournful lament that is suspended between acting out her trauma and an attempt to work through it, and invites comparison with what Kyo Maclear (2003) calls the "vexed impossibility of memory" and the "unstitched terror of remembering and witnessing" (238).

There are two narratives that occupy centre stage in Ernestina's attempt to construct a memory-narrative of the trauma of her daughter's "disappearance". The first is the story of Nokuthula's incessant crying as a baby. The second is a repetitive and almost obsessive quality in the way she draws out themes from her memory of Nokuthula. The latter reflects extreme emotional arousal that seems to suggest a failure of integration.

Nokuthula's childhood crying is something that dominated the Simelane household, and the households of extended family members. Efforts to cure her of her crying took Ernestina to paediatricians, spiritual healers, and traditional healers. It was a nightmarish mystery, Ernestina now says. As Nokuthula was her first child, when Ernestina could not find a cure, she was convinced that Nokuthula's crying had some purpose and meaning that transcended her painful and difficult experience as first-time mother. When Nokuthula was a toddler, and the crying subsided, a stubbornness emerged in her, which was to become part of her personality characteristic in her development into adulthood. That too, for Ernestina, *meant* something: Nokuthula "stubborn" in her inconsolable crying, and "stubborn" in her resoluteness and strength of ideas: for Ernestina, there must be a reason why she had to go through such a difficult time as a young mother.

Distress about Nokuthula's crying is not just a story about the challenges of a young mother with a child who would not stop crying. Its significance lies in its transformation into a signifier of things to come. And now, it seems, Ernestina has finally established its meaning—the unsolvable mystery of Nokuthula's crying then, as impenetrable as the mystery of her "disappearance" now.

The crying, while it represents an earlier struggle, is a less overwhelming memory. It was an experience that Ernestina describes as having been "nightmarish", but one that nevertheless can be organised into narrative memory—the story of Nokuthula's crying can be reconstructed and told from beginning to end. The story of Nokuthula's "disappearance" however, is something too overwhelming to face head-on. The "crying narrative" then, while it represents something that was profoundly disruptive for Ernestina, has taken on a new significance. Now it is a memory that stands in place of the one that defies understanding. In effect, it is an "evasion" of the unarticulated trauma of Nokuthula's "disappearance".

The name "Nokuthula" means "a state of calm", but the name seems to have brought Ernestina neither peace nor calm. When we give a person a name, we assign an identity that distinguishes the person from others through our daily use of the name. To name something is to know it, so the expression goes. But Nokuthula imbued her name with new meanings beyond the name itself. Ernestina remembers the drama of Nokuthula's childhood so vividly and painfully: unremitting crying, sleepless nights, emotional strife, and endless search for remedies. From infancy, Nokuthula marked herself out from the meaning that her name carried, and carved new symbolism from it whose significance was to go well beyond the crying years of her childhood. Today, that new meaning has become a sign that draws her family from the memory of that original site of grief and pain in the past, to the painful and relentless search for a daughter's whereabouts. The haunting quality of her absence is now registered through the haunting memory of her crying, as a presence.

Unlike her childhood crying, Nokuthula's "disappearance" defies any possibility of being infused with meaning, because it is unfinished trauma; it continues to exist as unresolved, unassimilated fragments of something extreme. We often refer to those who are left behind after a death of a loved one as "survivors": so and so is "survived" by her or his closest family members. People who are missing, however, have no survivors. The disappearance of loved ones leaves victims behind, loved ones caught up in a vortex of uncertainty, the prison of their own memory, forever paralysed between knowing and not knowing. Emotions are frozen in an internal dark zone of denial, a refusal to believe that one may never see one's loved one again. Ernestina struggles with this internal dynamic. To escape the conundrum, she reverts to the things she is certain about, objects that mark Nokuthula's life; objects that, in a sense, inject her presence in the face of her agonising absence.

Much attention is paid to verbal language as a vehicle for narrative representation. Yet body language, and other forms of symbolic expression, can also be ways of communicating difficult traumatic experience. When I first visited Ernestina in her home in Bethel for the shoot of the film *Betrayal,* I was struck by the intensity with which she talked about Nokuthula. Not only the talking: there was a lot of energy in the way she moved from her bedroom to the living room, and from the living room to the kitchen to fetch something or other that had belonged to Nokuthula, or that reminded her of Nokuthula. She was energetically, almost compulsively, moving back and forth, talking, explaining, bringing objects of Nokuthula's memory that she had stored in her bedroom: an album with Nokuthula's childhood photos, an old photograph from her university days, a clip from a newspaper with Nokuthula's picture, a stainless steel tea set that Nokuthula brought home during her last visit. Ernestina moved eagerly in and out between her bedroom, living room, kitchen, and dining room. The crockery that was going to be Nokuthula's birthday gift on that last fateful September before she was abducted and disappeared, still gift-wrapped in its original box; the dress that she would have worn for her graduation, the graduation gown—all symbols of an absent daughter whose presence was now evoked through the things that had been preserved, so it seemed, as if she would one day return.

There was a dramatic quality to Ernestina's movement in and out of the rooms in her house. The items she brought were memory artefacts, and the almost obsessive manner in which she laid them out on her dining room table symbolic of fragments of traumatic memory—the "unfinished business" of her trauma—a piecing together of what psychiatrists Van der Kolk and Van der Hart call the unintegrated "scraps of overwhelming experience" (1995: 176). This was Ernestina's attempt to retell the story of her missing daughter, a search for the meaning that would help place her trauma in some form of narrative.

Ernestina's energy and enthusiasm, and the unfolding story of her daughter told through the objects of memory that she brought into her living room seemed to be more about celebration than mourning—celebration of hope for Nokuthula's possible homecoming. At the same time, Ernestina's apparent determination to recapture her daughter's presence betrayed an underlying anxiety that she might never return. This raging terror within (hope-despair-hope) is the burden of many parents like Ernestina whose loved ones have never returned, and forever remain "missing". Thus, the objects of memory represent simultaneously the possible finality of Nokuthula's departure from their lives, and the hope of her re-entry into it. Either way, these memory objects were bestowed with profound affective investment.

In the items laid out we witnessed too the shrine-like effect of the objects. Nokuthula's face in the photographs, from her infancy, to school-days, to university life, represented the vibrancy and presence of a life cherished by her family. At the same time, her face represented the violence of her separation from her loved ones. The brutality of the system of apartheid was clearly evoked by a full-length picture of Nokuthula and next to it the tiny shack on the farm where her torturers imprisoned her. A huge front-page headline in the South African newspaper *The Sowetan* summarised Nokuthula's story in three words: MISSING IN ACTION[5]. Her smiling face seemed also to reflect the stubbornness that Ernestina talked about, rendering a certain sense of silent defiance of her own organisation, the ANC, which had failed to celebrate her heroic contribution. In this sense then, Nokuthula's "shrine" on her mother's table represented a *counter*-narrative: in the reports by her former commanders in Swaziland she was simply "a courier". Ernestina, in contrast, tells the story of a daughter who took major risks and played a critical role in the ANC's underground structures. No sound issued from the memory-objects that Ernestina laid out, yet they told a story that moved me deep down into the ravages of her unspeakable trauma.

Ernestina's traumatic loss, by its inarticulable nature, confines itself into what Saul Friedlander (1992) and others have termed "deep memory". It is "deep" because it remains essentially unassimilated. The depth of Ernestina's

[5] *The Sowetan*, 15 February 1995.

trauma is reflected in her difficulty to separate from Nokuthula, manifested in repeatedly addressing her younger daughter Thembi with Nokuthula's name. The repetitiveness with which this happened points to the distortion of reality, an avoidance of the hidden secrets that she is afraid of confronting.

Nokuthula's voice continues to cry out in Ernestina's memory. Her hope, it seems, is to redeem Nokuthula from the terrain of memory into real human presence. She has been waiting for answers; she wants ultimately to restore some coherence, to bring some finality to Nokuthula's story. The process of grieving presents us with a reflective ability to put the past in its proper place, and to move on. In the case of death of a loved one, this reflective process is assisted by rituals such as funerals. These rituals imply a clear end of a life. In their memory of the loved one, the surviving family members can anticipate a future without the loved one, a future of absence. There is *completion* in the mind, a clear understanding of the events and what one might call "closure" in one's memory. With the disappearance of a loved one, however, grief is boundless, and remains a deep, bottomless uncertainty. The time that has passed since Nokuthula's death suggests that her "disappearance" may be final. Yet how can Ernestina accept its finality when there are no mortal remains?

On the last day of filming of Nokuthula's story for the documentary *Betrayal*, we went, with Nokuthula's younger sister, Thembi, to the farm where Nokuthula had been kept prisoner and tortured. The farm, like so many like it where covert operations were conducted across South Africa, is a stark demonstration of the normalisation of violence sponsored by the apartheid state, where farms, often owned by family and friends of members of the security police, were transformed into sites of torture and murder. Here was a normal household, where normal everyday life carried on, while in the backyard an unspeakable gross human rights abuse was taking place—an abnormal place with an eerie feeling of normality. Was it possible that no one heard Nokuthula's cries? Did they turn a deaf ear to her pain-filled screaming? The magnitude of such calculated inhumanity overwhelms the mind's ability to comprehend the cruelty visited upon Nokuthula.

Thembi, Nokuthula's younger sister, who has taken the baton from her father (who died before he could know the truth about his daughter) and from her mother to continue the quest to find the truth about Nokuthula, burst into tears when we entered the tiny shack where the torturers had detained her sister. I thought to myself: This is the site of pain. This is where Nokuthula's tragedy began and ended. Perhaps this is where Ernestina's endless conflict and hope for her daughter's return will be buried. "A room with buried secrets" came to my mind; walls infused with unspeakable truths. But for Ernestina the moment of truth has never come. Not even through the TRC, where she and her family spent days hoping that at last they would know what happened to Nokuthula.

Ironically, the TRC seemed like an endless moment of *absence* of truth itself. The only truth, it seemed, were the tears of Nokuthula's mother, now shed by Thembi. Will Thembi's children cry her tears too? That is the single most disturbing legacy of unsolved disappearances. It is testament to the realities of the trauma of the disappearance of a loved one, and its trans-generational consequences in the lives of those left behind.

Nokuthula's story reminds us how people who cannot find the body of a deceased person need a lot of psychological help to find ways of connecting to the loved one without becoming too dependent on finding the missing body—to build other symbols that could help them continue the process of healing. It could be something that represents the body, something that is not tangible, but exists only in symbolic form. It might for instance take the form of a ritual with people who share some memories of the missing person with the family—people who can help the family to recognise what was lost and celebrate the memory in a way that marks the person's life, not as a life that is dependent on finding a body, but as a life that remains in their memories, and in the memories of others. Rituals give those who have not found the body of their deceased loved one something to hold onto. If the memory is of the tragic event that caused the death but celebrates the life of the lost one, that memory becomes the representation of the body. So what is "found" is the representation of the life, even though not the material body; the ritual ceremony embodies the presence of the lost loved one, even in the absence of the physical body.

What complicates closure in the case of Nokuthula, is the fact that her family does not know for certain whether she was a traitor or a hero, for there was conflicting evidence: she was described as loyal unto death to the liberation struggle but also (by one who said he spoke as a witness) as a collaborator with the apartheid government. So the parents do not actually know of whom they are taking leave. These are the complex questions that come into play in many cases of gross human rights violation committed in the context of struggle. Should the loved one be remembered as a hero or as a traitor? Part of the healing process of memorialisation, the ritual ceremony, is about writing that memory. Even if there is no clarity, somehow it should be ensured that the celebration of the memory remembers the "disappeared" person as a hero—for the sake of the healing of the remaining family members. There must be no ambiguity. If the ritual repeats the ambiguities, the grieving family is retraumatised, but if the ritual somehow allows the family members to find a heroic memory, they can become whole again.

People may argue that, because everybody has something of a hero as well as a villain in him, one could celebrate the humanity of the deceased person, encompassing good as well as bad memories. The ultimate goal of the therapist is to help the grieving person acknowledge that the deceased may have had some blemishes—even serious ones—but still to love and accept them, and grieve for the loss. But the therapist should not push to achieve that acknowledgement too soon; the feelings of the grieving person, struggling with the pain of loss, may be too tender to carry the extra burden of accepting the deceased's 'sins'. The focus should be on healing. The therapist therefore needs to focus as much as possible on issues that emphasise the good parts in the whole event. Once the family has transcended the mourning and the hate, they can be open to the possibility that there is always good and bad in every person, something of the villain and something of the hero.

The crying voices of South Africa

Nokuthula's history is an example of the difficulties faced by a family in attempting to reach closure; but in a broader context, it could also be seen as a metaphor for the painful legacy of South Africa's past—a past full of voices crying to be heard, of unfinished business crying for closure. Although it is impossible to reach full knowledge of the past, and although final closure will always be out of our reach, these crying voices urge us towards the ideals of knowing and working through the past. The voices pose a challenge for oral and literary historians, for narrative therapists and creative writers—ultimately for all of us—to hear and to tell the stories of those unheard, to give a voice to those who have been silenced. In the following paragraphs, two relevant matters in the highly complex issue of the unheard voices of our history are discussed: making public spaces intimate, and the role of forgiveness.

Making public spaces intimate

"Making public spaces intimate" means bringing our most intimate hurts into the public space, so that the "talking about the hurts" triggers something in the audience with which they identify, which they receive and respond to. So when you express your pain, you are expressing it in the name of all of those others who find a place in your heart to connect to with your story. Your story becomes the story also of others present, so my reaction, and your reaction to my story is also *our* reaction. When we embrace the story, we are embracing it with a mutual feeling of connectedness. The consequence of that embrace is the hope that we need so badly, so that we can move forward after all our traumas.

Let me illustrate this with an example. A while ago, I (P G-M) took a number of students to the Cape Town Holocaust Centre, where they were addressed by an old German woman, a survivor from Auschwitz. She mentioned that she did not see herself as a victim any more; that she wanted to forgive and transcend the anger and hatred of the past, so that she could end her life with inner peace and leave a legacy of reconciliation to her children. One of the students, a young German, went to her afterwards and spoke to her in German. Whereas German visitors to the Holocaust Centre normally are ashamed to acknowledge that they are German, this student was clearly, through his language, identifying with the past of his people, admitting their guilt and appreciating the woman's forgiveness. She came to him, extended her hand, touched his shoulder, and they started conversing in German. Although the others present could not understand the German, the message of guilt and forgiveness, of acknowledgement and reconciliation, was clear to everyone, and they were all deeply touched by what happened. A public space had been made intimate.

One could argue that this young German was innocent of the sins of the fathers, and had no need to apologise. However, we must remind the reader of the quote from Alasdair MacIntyre in chapter 1. According to MacIntyre, the legacy from the past constitutes

> the given of my life, my moral starting point … I am born with a past; and to try to cut myself off from that past, in the individualistic mode, is to deform my present relationships. The possession of an historical identity and the possession of a social identity coincide. Notice that rebellion against my identity is always one possible mode of expressing it. (MacIntyre 1981: 205)

Seen in this light, collective guilt is not a fact, but a choice; and linking oneself to one's past opens up the possibility of vicarious apology and of rectifying the wrongs of previous generations. History is healed, as it were.

A place where this is happening, according to Sean Field, is the District Six Museum in Cape Town:

> The museum helped ex-residents who were forcibly removed under apartheid to gain land restitution and through vibrant museum spaces, with evocative visual and oral history exhibits, the community is being regenerated … Through a public education programme and frequent visits by descendents, university and school groups, the museum sustains trans-generational dialogues and contributes to the 'post-memories' of the following generations. (Field 2006: 40–41)

More and more, in places where there has been massive trauma—places where massive healing is needed—state and church and community organisations need to organise public occasions where reconciliation can be fostered. On a smaller scale, individuals should organise meetings between small groups from different backgrounds to share their stories with one another. However, we must be aware of possible problems and obstacles. Often, after a promising start, such meetings stagnate, and those involved become bored, and unwilling to continue the process. This resistance is natural; it is always difficult to do something new, something unheard of. Trust has been shattered in the past, and is not easily recovered—we are full of memories that divide, negative associations, and stereotypes. We also have different experiences in life—for instance, some people may never have left a township, others never entered one. So the process will be a long one, needing lots of patience and endurance.

At a certain stage there will be a need to stop focusing on the stories of the past, and to start looking forward together. C S Lewis said, if you want a friend, look for a common interest. In South Africa, at the moment, at the beginning of this period of meeting, we need the eyes of victims and perpetrators to be turned to each other as they face each other for the first time; but when they have gone through that stage, they should turn their eyes towards a common goal or interest and say, "Now let us do something together."

The role of forgiveness

The concept that most clearly symbolises hope for the future in our traumatised South Africa, is the concept of forgiveness. Forgiveness brings an end to the repetitive cycle of violation. In the words of Julia Kristeva:

> Forgiveness is ahistorical. It breaks the concatenation of causes and effects, crimes and punishment, it stays the time of actions. A strange space opens up in a timelessness that is not one of the primitive unconscious, desiring and murderous, but its counterpart—its sublimation with full knowledge of the facts, a loving harmony that is aware of its violences but accommodates them, elsewhere. (Kristeva 1989: 200)

> Forgiveness seems to say … I allow you to make a new person of yourself. So that the unconscious might inscribe itself in a new narrative that will not be the eternal return of the death drive in the cycle of crime and punishment, it must pass through the love of forgiveness, be transferred to the love of forgiveness. (204)

There is no price that will ever be adequate to pay people who have been ruptured and traumatised. What is necessary, therefore, is finding a new language that will bring us together—the language of forgiveness. We talk about reparation and compensation, and that is important, but at some stage we need to come to a place where we let go of the desire for retribution and revenge. Until we come to that place, we will be carrying the anger and the resentment that drive us in our communication with others. The anger may be justified, and indeed we should be angry and resentful against those who hurt us, but if we harbour these feelings indefinitely, we pay a heavy price. Bear in mind that these feelings of revenge and the return of anger are carried on from one generation to the next, so that the hate is not just my hate, but my children's hate as well. We must reach a moment where we take stock and face what happened and then move forward with a new urgency. That urgency is forgiveness.

By forgiveness we do not mean that we should forget; we do not even mean that we should forgive and say, "Now let's be buddies and love one another." We see forgiveness as something that opens up a new way of relating to our traumas. Trauma can drive people to feelings of resentment, to hate, to revenge. By forgiveness we mean a new position that invites us to relate to our trauma in a different way, a way that allows others to come into our space and to be in relation with us—instead of repeating the hatred that was imposed on us. We let go of the desire for revenge for the benefit of our children and for our own benefit, so that we can move freely, and be relieved of the imprisoning feelings of hate and vengeance.

How forgiveness relates to justice is a complex question. Forgiveness and justice are not diametrically opposed to each other. When we reflect on the notion of justice, particularly in relation to human rights abuses, we need to think of justice not as an end in itself, but as a process. In that process we should strive towards a critical balance between justice and compassion. This is particularly important when we consider how to heal past traumas and when the victims and the perpetrators will be living together as neighbours. The idea of simply meting out justice, a legalistic form of justice that seeks retribution, does not deal with the question of how people live together as neighbours after a time of atrocities. The ideal is a balance between compassion and justice.

The notion of forgiveness often evokes in people ideas of forgetting or of just allowing people to go free. It is important that we do not imagine forgiveness as something that we can prescribe. Justice is something that is prescribed. People commit crimes, and they must be prosecuted. That is the prescriptive way of responding to atrocities. But we cannot respond in that way with forgiveness. People who have been hurt or lost loved ones, need time. They may not be able to embrace forgiveness for some time. They need time to mourn their loss.

The process of mourning does include feelings of anger and revenge. People are angry and they want to hit back—and that can be explained: when people are hurt and violated as a result of actions by other human beings, it often leaves a feeling of humiliation and loss. One's power, one's sense of control has been taken away, so anger and revenge are really about reclaiming one's sense of power and one's sense of control, and dealing with the effect of humiliation. Humiliation makes us helpless and powerless, and when we are angry and revengeful, we are active, we replace those feelings of humiliation. We say, "I want to do something to the other person. I want to grab him and I want to hurt him." But that is also the danger of this process. You are still a victim because you are a captive of both the victimiser and your own feelings. The feelings of anger and hatred take on a life of their own; they become our identity. Letting go of those feelings can seem like another loss because you are now losing your second identity.

Forgiveness allows people to have a new relationship with their trauma; it is a liberating act, a choice for freedom. Some people ask, why should victims be free of their anger and hatred? Why should we promote this kind of freedom from anger? It has been proven that forgiveness helps the victim to heal. The freedom from being captive to anger and hatred as a result of the trauma liberates people to embark on a new journey of healing.

CHAPTER FOUR

LITERARY NARRATIVES AND TRAUMA

The dream

A young girl, who was living with her mother, in a relationship in which she was badly abused, had the following dream:

"As far as I remember, I had this dream when I was sixteen, during a pretty stressful time. The interesting thing about it (to me) was that it was as though I was watching a film of some sort; only it was half real, half film. You know the way films work, that what is really happening is that you are seeing twenty-four stills per second, but that the still shots, when moved at that rate, give the illusion of movement on a screen. Well, when the dream started, I was looking at photographs of a crime scene being tossed onto a table while a news report in the background said that a woman had been stabbed repeatedly by her husband. He'd taken a knife to her and there was pretty much nothing left of her. The photographs being tossed onto the table were of that crime scene, the woman's body. They were being tossed faster and faster until eventually the images started moving and the scene in the photographs came to life.

"The woman was lying on a bed in a dingy room with only a dim bluish light. The room was hardly bigger than a bathroom with one iron bed and a television in it, that's all. The blue light was coming from the television, which was playing the news report. There were police all over the room, examining her. She was lying on the bed and had been pretty much sliced to pieces. There were deep horizontal wounds all the way up her body in zigzags, and she had long dark hair that was falling over the edge of the bed. Her skin was bluish from the television. She was very thin, as though she had been suffering for a long time before she was killed. I presumed she was living in this room because she had made some attempt to leave, but had been killed later for leaving.

"I was in the room as well, but I think more like a ghost, I don't think I really mattered in that scene. Although the news reports and police seemed to be under the impression that she'd been dead for some time, I was aware that the woman was very much alive still, although she had been hurt so badly that nobody else could tell. For some reason I had a kind of connection to her and could feel that she was still alive, but when I tried to speak, it was as though none of the police could hear me or see me. I was trying to tell them that she was still alive, so that they would stop prodding her, because they weren't being very gentle (as one isn't, I suppose, with a dead body: this is the problem with being dead—no-one really feels pressed to be gentle with you any more) and I was sure they were hurting her very badly, although she couldn't say it herself. I was eventually screaming and screaming for them to realise she was alive before they took her away and dismissed her as dead, but they didn't hear.

"Eventually the police left—though I seem to remember them still being somewhere around, just not visible—and a rat crawled out of the corner of the room and ran up her body. It used the wounds as footholds. It climbed all the way up to her face, then sat still for a minute or two on her cheek before it dug its claws into her eyes and started eating. All this time I was screaming for the police to come and take the rat away, because she was alive and I knew she could feel it, but they didn't come back and I couldn't scare the rat away and I ended up just watching till it had eaten all of her eyes and there was nothing left.

"For me the biggest horror of this was the helplessness of not being heard, no matter how loudly I felt I was screaming. I've had a lot of dreams on this theme; always having something terribly important to say but it just isn't there or it just isn't heard, or no-one seems to understand the words I'm saying. Another recurring theme is the dream of a corpse I have eaten, that is still alive, and I have to either kill it, swallow it, or force it back into my stomach to stop it from speaking. I think it's also a common nightmare we all have, of being taken for dead when we are very much alive, and can still feel just like everybody else, even if we aren't conscious or strong enough to say so. I don't think I'll ever forget having to stand there and just watch a rat gnaw through the eyes of a still living woman, without being able to do anything, for as long as I live."

In the dream, the girl is split into two figures—she is the "I" of the dream, the onlooker, representing the ego; but she is also the sliced-up woman, clearly a projection of the suppressed, suffering part inside her. The "I" of the dream, with whom the dreaming girl identifies, mentions that "I had some kind of connection with her"; she is the only one close enough to the woman to realise that she, though badly wounded, is still alive and has some feeling left in her. The split in two is typical of traumatised people and indicates a dissociation of the ego from the suffering self, in order to create a distance from the intense pain that is being experienced; it is a desperate way of trying to save the little life remaining in her by taking leave of the part of her which is being killed. The woman (the abused part of the self) is wounded, "sliced to pieces"—the wounds are a clear sign of trauma (indeed, the word trauma comes from the Greek word for "wound") and her being cut to pieces is an indication of her falling apart inwardly. She is kept in a little room which has all the qualities of a prison. The prison is bad, but trying to escape makes it worse, for when she tried to escape from it, she was severely punished.

The mother is disguised in the dream as an abusive husband; the disguise hides the painful fact that the mother who should be the caring one, acts in the same criminal way as the abusive husband in the television film. The husband's cruel behaviour is followed by some more cruelty towards the woman in the dream—this time by a rat. The rat uses the woman's wounds as footholds—it makes use of her pain and weak points to realise its aim of eating her eyes. It goes for one of the most sensitive and vital parts of the body—when the eyes are gone, blindness would be a step closer to death. The rat in the dream is a condensed figure: it could be seen as another disguise of the mother, where the contemptible behaviour towards the daughter is symbolised in a despicable animal; it could also be seen as those in society who make use of her weakness to suck her dry; or it could be interpreted as the daily demands made on the suffering girl, for which she has no strength.

The important message of the dream, that which the girl desperately wants to communicate, is that the woman, though badly wounded, is still alive. This indicates that the dreaming girl is conscious of the suffering she is going through, although she is suppressing the knowledge. Although she suppresses it, she also wants to communicate her message, a message with a positive and a negative side to it. The bad part of the message is that the woman feels the intense pain of being abused; the good part is that she can still be saved, because she is not dead. Her experience of pain is a proof that she is alive. However, no-one seems to hear or understand the girl's urgent cries. The police who are failing her represent figures of authority: for instance the absent father, the divorce court, the family advocate and social workers, her school, etc. They are the ones who should protect "the woman", who should bring order into the chaos, who should catch the guilty "husband" and see to it that "he" is punished; but they are blind and deaf to the dream girl's desperate calls for help. As a matter of fact, they make the woman's pain worse by their insensitive prodding. "Prodding" also suggests cruel questions and suggestions, to try and force her to come to life and react in the way which they expect of her, but they do not get to the heart of the matter: that she is still alive and feeling the pain of her wounds as well as of their "prodding". Because she does not react in the way they demand they do not realise how much pain their prodding is causing her; they easily declare her to be "dead", that is, not in need of further attention. And so, without coming to an understanding of the situation or providing a solution to the problem, the police leave. Thereby the last thread of hope for the woman and the on-looking girl disappears. The woman is left to her fate of being slowly finished off by a rat, and the girl has to watch it happen.

The other recurrent theme in the suffering girl's dreams is that of "a corpse I have eaten, that is still alive, and I have to either kill it, swallow it, or force it back into my stomach to stop it from speaking." The link with the first-mentioned dream is obvious: both are symbolic representations of an inner death. Feeling pain is a positive sign of life, but when the pain becomes unbearable, the only way out is a denial of all feeling, an inner numbness that relieves the pain but is also a symptom of inward death. There is a double shame suggested here: of being a corpse and of eating a corpse – that is, of being "dead" and of acknowledging it. The outside world, demanding "normality", does not want to know about unbearable pain, inner numbness and death; we tend to ostracise the one who is "different". The problem is therefore not only the inward dying process, but the impossibility of communicating it.

Contemplating the dream of the sliced-up woman, the girl concludes that her being eaten by a rat was not the worst part of the dream, as one might have imagined—"the biggest horror of this was the helplessness of not being heard". So much of what this book is about comes to the fore in this dream: the pain, not only of being bodily and mentally wounded, but the helplessness of not being able to communicate it. The wounded woman symbolises the unsaved traumatised person as well as the suppressed part of the psyche that needs to be acknowledged by the ego and by the outside world. The on-looking girl represents the urgent need to be heard and understood; being understood would indeed be an essential part of being saved. But the outsiders, like the friends of Job, prod the trauma victim into telling the kind of story they want to hear; the victim therefore has no way of revealing her real situation. Not only have others failed to open themselves up to the horror of the trauma experience, but everyday language is also insufficient to express it.

The complex relationship between reality and textuality is significant. The girl dreamt that she "was watching a film of some sort; only it was half real, half film". This film is a news report, that is, a factual representation on screen of something that really happened (though here it is part of a dream). So the girl is doubly protected from an atrocity that really happened (her being abused)—by the distancing of a television screen and by the "unreality" of a dream. The photographs of the crime that she looks at are also only representations of what happened, not the real happening. But then, in a dramatic turn in events, the television story and the photographs come to life and form part of the on-looking girl's "real" experience. However, the dreaming girl is once more doubly protected from the painful truth of her being abused by her mother: by the symbolic disguises of the dream narrative, and by the fact that it is "only" a dream. And yet, reality shines through, a reality that the subconscious is aware of but which consciousness does not want to acknowledge. The dream narrative, though disguising the content of its message, is so vivid that it remains in the memory and demands attention.

In many ways, dream narratives are like literary narratives, on which this chapter focuses. Literary narratives reveal, as well as conceal, trauma; real life issues are disguised in fictional characters and situations. Like the dream narrative, literary narrative shows the tension between disclosure and silence—as discussed in chapter 2. But, whereas the dream is a private matter, the literary narrative is public domain, inviting public discussion. But literary narratives have so many facets that we easily miss an essential part of them: their content of traumas with the resulting possibilities of resonance in everyday life.

The shattering of mental schemes

Experience is normally processed in the memory in the form of a narrative. This process includes the selection of relevant data, the construction of causal chains, the connection of events to characters, the episodic organisation of events, and the drawing of conclusions to make sense from an event and guide future behaviour (Wigren 1994: 415–416.) In contrast, traumatic memories leave the victim speechless; they "come back as emotional and sensory states with little verbal representation" (Van der Kolk 1996: 296). Traumatic memories are so overwhelming that they cannot be turned into narratives; they are usually triggered by associations; and they remain unassimilated in the psyche, accompanied by intense emotions, vivid images, nightmares and somatic symptoms such as sweating palms.

Normally, people make sense of new events by fitting them into pre-existing narrative mental schemes. Severe trauma cannot be contained in these schemes and shatters their foundations; it defies all attempts to ascribe meaning to the traumatic experience.

> Traumatic memories are the unassimilated scraps of overwhelming experiences, which need to be integrated with existing mental schemes, and be transformed into narrative language. (Van der Kolk 1995: 176)

When such integration has taken place, the story of the event can be told, the flashbacks and the somatic symptoms disappear, and the person regains control over the past. Integration can be achieved either by adapting the trauma to fit into the scheme, or by adapting the scheme to contain the trauma, or both.

Ernst van Alphen emphasises the linguistic nature of the mental schemes into which experience is fitted; he points out that they are based on the discourse available in the relevant culture. To van Alphen, an event becomes experience only when it is fitted into the patterns of existing discourses; trauma is "failed experience" because it cannot fit into the schemes of these discourses (Van

Alphen 1999: 25–26). In an analysis of Lawrence Langer's *Holocaust Testimonies,* Van Alphen distinguishes four kinds of problems that Holocaust victims had when attempting to talk about their traumatic experiences:

1. In the language available to them, they had to refer to themselves as either subject or object of the actions that had taken place in the camps, but they felt that neither of these perspectives was appropriate. They were confused about whether they were agents who had to take responsibility for what had happened or passive victims of the cruelty taking place. In their confusion, many split themselves in two and imagined that all of it was happening to someone else.

2. For some Holocaust victims, "the situation was defined by the *lack* of choice. One just followed humiliating impulses that killed one's subjectivity but safeguarded one's life" (Van Alphen 1999: 31). In the discourse they used before the camp experience, selfishness was deemed bad and unselfishness was good—but in the camps, selfishness was the condition for survival. In Western society, inaction in a horrible situation is identified with cowardice; but in the camps there seemed no possibility for action that could make a difference. They felt totally powerless, and found it difficult to formulate this situation in conventional Western discourses.

3. In everyday experience, every event is linked to other events preceding it, and evokes expectations of other events to follow. Van Alphen uses the example of the writing of an examination—it is preceded by preparation and study, and opens up future possibilities such as a career, or the opportunity for further study. In contrast, in Auschwitz, there was no such sense of continuity; no-one understood the circumstances that had led to their being in the camp or what they could expect from the future, because they had no other experience to which they could relate it. "Life in the camps in all its aspects had no precedent" (Van Alphen 1999: 33).

4. Auschwitz survivors found it impossible to communicate the horror of the Holocaust in a conventional narrative with a beginning, middle and end. Their Holocaust past was still with them, overwhelming their minds and determining their lives, and this experience could not be communicated in a narrative framework distinguishing clearly between present, past and future. To them, their liberation could not serve as "closure" of the camp narrative; they found that their feeling of being dead while still alive was simply not narratable.

Van Alphen concludes that trauma remains "failed experience" as long as it is unassimilated by the mental schemes created for making sense of events. This has consequences not only for the individual, who cannot incorporate what happened into his personal history, but also for society at large, whose collective history is distorted by the omission. "Experiences are … collectively shared because they are grounded on cultural discourses; this shared background makes experiences and memories 'sharable'" (Van Alphen 1999: 37). Without the integration of traumatic events into cultural discourses, individuals as well as society in general stay traumatised.

Bibliotherapy

In the renewal of cultural discourses and the exploration of the possibilities of language to contain new experience, literary writers have a vital role to play. They are the pioneers of language, continually searching for the appropriate words and narrative structures to communicate personal and collective issues. They are challenged by new, unheard of experience, and stretch language to its limits and beyond, often breaking down conventional narrative structures in order to create new, original ways of communicating the seemingly incommunicable.

In dealing with trauma, writers can, vicariously, express what other trauma victims find impossible to tell. Readers, in the reading and interpretation of literary narratives, can in a way become creative writers as well by "re-creating" the narratives in their own minds—organising the elements of the story into a coherent whole, internalising it and applying it to their own situation. Literary narratives can help a traumatised person to confront suppressed feelings. When victims find it too hard to confront their trauma directly and to talk openly about it, literature can provide a way of facing it indirectly—partly acknowledging and partly disguising their trauma—and of talking indirectly about their trauma by discussing the literary narrative.

A psychologist from Bloemfontein, P J Rossouw, used "bibliotherapy" in his treatment of soldiers suffering from post-traumatic stress disorder after the "Border Wars" in South Africa in the 1970s and 1980s. He used a number of literary texts about these wars to show the patients that they were not abnormal in their reactions to the war. These literary texts, in contrast with the official war propaganda of government and army officers, depicted the futility of the war, the anxiety and depression of many soldiers, and the shared humanity of the armies fighting each other. Patients were asked to read the texts and write down their own reactions to them. With the help of these literary texts, ex-soldiers were able to acknowledge their own suppressed doubts and anxieties, and could be led to new ways of looking at their enemies of the past. The aim of the treatment was "cognitive restructuring"—breaking down negative perceptions of the past and enabling the ex-soldiers to look differently at themselves, at their fellow human beings and at their country. Thus they were detraumatised and prepared for the radical changes that would come to the country with the end of the war and the abolition of apartheid (Rossouw 2001: 33–60).

Rossouw emphasises that the therapist should know the patient well before prescribing a literary text to him or her, and should also know the text well, to ensure that it is relevant to the patient's situation. Furthermore, the patient should never be forced to read anything, and should not receive too much reading matter, since this could make him or her despondent. In addition, the patient's intellectual capacity should always be taken into account (2001: 45).

The patients treated by Rossouw were people severely suffering from post-traumatic stress. However, the links between literary narratives and trauma are not confined to these extreme cases. The phenomenon of trauma, characterised generally by the falling apart of a life narrative, contains a continuum of experiences, ranging from an overwhelming trauma, which leaves the victim speechless with horror, to the smaller crises of everyday life where goals are missed and ambitions can be shattered. Furthermore, traumas are characterised by wounds and divisions in the psyche *and* in society at large. As far as the traumatisation of a society goes, the divisions can range from civil war to cold distrust and alienation between the cultural groups. Literary narratives can play a vital role in the working through and healing of these different kinds of trauma—of being wounded and of losing the plot of life.

It should be emphasised that we do not necessarily regard pleasant stories with happy endings and positive messages as appropriate material for working through trauma. Trauma victims would probably experience these narratives as false, and might react with aggression to them. On the other hand, stories that seem gruelling could ring true to them, and validate their own experience.

Art as a vehicle of trauma

Although this book focuses on the role of literary narratives in working through trauma, it should be emphasised that much of what is said here could also be applied to other forms of artistic narrative: the narratives of film and drama; the "stories" told by paintings and sculpture; or in music; or in artistic expressions where these art forms are combined, for example in films with music. However, a fuller exploration of this theme would be the material for another book.

To stimulate further discussion and study, let us then briefly mention a number of qualities typical of the literary narrative which make it extremely useful as a vehicle for the expression and discussion of trauma. Here we are looking at the matter not from the perspective of the writer indirectly expressing his or her traumas (that is a different, also very important issue), but from the perspective of the reader "re-creating" the narrative in his or her own mind.

1. Indirect confrontation and expression of trauma

When trauma victims find it too painful to confront their own traumas, they may discover a literary character or characters with whom they can identify and thus indirectly confront their own trauma. The fact that the character traits and the traumatic situation are not quite the same as the reader's, but show some similarity, makes the painful identification more bearable. Once identification has taken place, the trauma of the reader can be vicariously expressed through the narrative, and the reading can bring about a catharsis of suppressed emotions. Healing possibilities are thus linked to an increase in insight and an expression of pain. Furthermore, literary narratives may give traumatised readers, isolated by overwhelming trauma, some validation of their own experience.

In many novels, we find a polyphony of voices—the characters have unique voices, differentiating them from one another, and all of them from the narrator. Modern novelists tend to shy away from authoritarian narrators dictating the run of events and explicating the appropriate reaction to the story—independence is granted to every character. This polyphony of voices in the novel leaves the reader with a wide variety of possible identifications.

2. From chaos to structure

Turning trauma into literary narrative means turning chaos into structure. A narrative has a topic, and normally keeps to that point; the plot of the story usually creates a causal link between different events; characters act according to their identities, and their actions show some kind of continuity; and patterns are created and repeated to indicate central themes. In all these ways, the shattering effect of the trauma is transformed by the author into (relative) coherence and unity. Even in a novel where the identity of the characters and the continuity of the plot are deliberately undermined to suggest a loss of coherence, this "disorderly" pattern is, paradoxically, also a pattern, appropriate for the specific theme. A reader whose life has lost all meaning, whose narrative has been shattered, may thus find a story that fits her situation. In the writer's appropriate expression of the theme, a meaningful language structure is created that can be appropriated by the reader. The form thus given to the formlessness of trauma, is an antidote to despair, and suggests that some meaning is still to be found, even in desperate situations. The beauty of literature lies in the unity of theme and structure; it is a beauty that possesses a healing potential within itself, regardless of the content of the narrative.

3. Imagining new possibilities

Literary narratives may contain suggestions of how to respond meaningfully to trauma. Literary characters typically meet with challenges and catastrophes which do not leave them unchanged. Often a literary character develops through his trauma into (in Coleridge's words) "a sadder and a wiser man". His old identity, his conventional assumptions and expectations, may have been shattered and he has to adapt to new circumstances. In the imagining of new ways of survival and in the rewriting of identities, the literary writer is often a pioneer; and the traumatised reader, suffering from a shattered identity, may find guidance in the literary narrative.

4. Healing a divided society

In a traumatised society, scarred by divisions, collective anger and animosity, writers have a vital role to play. South African writers could be expected to act almost as their own Truth and Reconciliation Commission, creating writing relevant to the needs of their own recently traumatised society and working towards the reconciliation of their people. People should listen carefully to what such writers have to say.

Writers could help with the search for truth and reconciliation in various ways:

(a) The writer has to make a "diagnosis" of the country, revealing not only what is good, but also what is lacking. Writers long for a better world, and this desire tends to lead their focus to wrongs that should be rectified: to violence and rape, to suffering and a lack of empathy, to poverty, and to the lust for power. Readers often do not like this and blame the messenger when the news is bad; they want their writers to praise the country and glorify its people. However, the first step to the healing of a society is to take literary writers seriously when they reveal misery and evil; readers should try to link what is suggested in the writers' texts to everyday life, and move towards making right what is being shown as wrong.

(b) Marginalised people are often the focus of the writer's attention. The writer acts as representative of the silent and the oppressed; those who are powerless are often found at the centre of novels, and those who are silenced by society are heard in literature, providing more privileged readers with an opportunity to expand their consciousness and deepen their sympathy. The writer calls our attention to "shadow figures" who need to be integrated into society; this forms, on a macro scale, a parallel to the individual healing process whereby the suppressed parts of the subconscious are integrated into consciousness.

(c) Our natural tendency is to feel threatened by what is different, and to form negative stereotypes of those who belong to another group—racial, cultural or religious. On the whole we like to believe that we are right and that everything that deviates from our norms, is wrong. Literature frequently destroys these stereotypes and challenges readers' imagination and empathy, stimulating them to discover a shared humanity in characters who are "different". In divided societies, people form different narratives of the past and the present; literature often combines these opposing narratives into one story, and introduces readers to the "other side" of society. hold sway

In the second half of the twentieth century for instance, when the apartheid government was ruling South Africa, Afrikaans writers played an important part in the breaking down of negative stereotyping by Afrikaners of "the others", and helped to prepare their readers for the normalisation of society (see Van der Merwe 1994). In Afrikaans stories about the "Border Wars", the attitudes of soldier characters often change when they come close to an enemy and meet him as a fellow human being. These stories, undermining the status quo, are examples of the tendency of writers to go against convention in their portrayal of "good" and "evil", revealing that much evil is done in the name of "goodness" and much that is feared as evil, is not.

5. The specific and the universal

In literary narratives, we find a unique combination of the specific and the universal. In this respect, literature differs from historiography. The difference lies not so much in the factuality of history and the fictionality of literature but in the ways in which they narrate about the outside world. Like Ricœur, we believe in "the referential claims of both history and fiction … the claim to be *about* something" (Ricœur 1983: 5). Historical and literary narratives are both stories about the world, but they are narrated in different ways: historiography needs historical evidence, whereas "fictional narratives … ignore the burden of providing evidences of that kind" (5). Similarly to Aristotle, Ricœur believes that literature, "not being the slave of the real event, can address itself directly to the universal, i.e., to what a certain kind of person would likely or necessarily do" (16).

Certain themes which are of central importance to the literary narrative, themes such as death, trauma and pain—themes on which we too are focusing—are experiences universally known to humanity. Because literature deals with universal themes it is comprehensible to a wide variety of readers. That is why the canonical works of literature are translated into many languages and read by many nations, and also by successive generations. Furthermore, great literary narratives leave their influence on later authors and thus form part of a large intertextual network touching the lives of ever more readers. The ability of the literary narrative to reach a multitude of people is one of its greatest strengths.

In the specific events of the literary narrative, universal themes are embedded. The task of the reader is to extricate general themes from specific literary scenes, and then apply these general themes to his or her specific situation. In a literary text there is a constant interaction, a mutual osmosis, between the specific and the universal. Analysing a literary narrative involves a search for the universal, essential aspects of life as revealed in the specific story; and thereafter a search for connections between these fundamental themes and the specific reader and his community. The significance of a story "wells up from *the intersection of the world of the text and the world of the reader*", says Ricœur;[6] and the reader's "configuration" of the text (putting the parts together) should lead to the "reconfiguration" of his life—that is, the reorganisation of his life in the light of the assimilated text (Ricœur 1991: 430).

Appropriation of the text is a vital part of reading literature. For different readers, a narrative will have greater or less relevance; the relevance will also be different for the same person at different stages of her life. Maybe our ideal should not necessarily be to read more literature, but rather to read more thoroughly when we do read it, not neglecting the important task of finding a personal and communal significance in what we read. If that cannot be found, the text should rather be left alone—it may reveal its relevance at a later stage.

Important for our discussion here, is the fact that literary narratives, through dealing with universal themes, can have a unifying function in a divided community. They bind authors to readers and different readers to each other; they communicate to a multitude of readers across the gulfs that divide them; they provide a shared basis for dialogue. Canonical texts that most people know and to which they can refer in their discussions, can therefore play a unifying role in society. Readers' interpretations and appropriations may differ, but they are all based on the same narratives, which thus form a link between the readers. Containing universal themes, but with a different applicability for each reader, the literary narrative confirms the unique identities of the readers as well as their communal bonds. In chapter 5, we further discuss the connections between the general ideas and the individual applicability of a literary text.

To wound or to heal?

In the foregoing paragraphs we focused on the healing potential of the literary narrative, but the question could rightly be asked of whether the function of literature should be to heal, or perhaps rather to wound. Should the literary narrative not break down oppressive structures and false assurances; should it not confront the readers with the fate of the suffering and let them share some of the pain? Should literature soothe us, or should it wake us from our insensitivity? Perhaps literature has a dual function, of wounding as well as healing; it heals, but partly through wounding. If our aim is to become people

---

[6] Reminder: all quoted emphasis is original unless noted otherwise.

with empathy, then suffering may be part of the healing process, as was argued in chapter 1.

Writers on trauma have noted the link between knowledge and pain. Reading texts of trauma, Dominick LaCapra argues, has an "unsettling dimension, whereby one is able to see things or ask questions that were not available to oneself or others in the past." He connects traumatic effects with "the very ability to learn from an exchange with the past" (LaCapra 1994: 27).

Maurice Blanchot, too, makes a connection between understanding and pain:

> To see properly is essentially to die. It is to introduce into sight the turning back which is ecstasy and which is death. This does not mean that everything sinks into the void. On the contrary, things then offer themselves in the inexhaustible fecundity of their meaning which our vision ordinarily misses—our vision which is capable of one point of view. (Blanchot 1982: 151)

In a very illuminating way, Shoshana Felman writes about the crisis of unsettlement which a group of students experienced when they attended her lectures on texts about trauma, including two texts about the Holocaust (Felman 1995: 13–60). Felman diagnosed the students' initial response to the texts as "an *anxiety of fragmentation*" (51); she realised that the class "*passed through its own answerlessness*" (53). She then invited them to write about their personal reactions to the discussed texts—wanting each student thereby to reaffirm his or her unique identity, the uniqueness of each person which was denied by the Nazis. She wanted the class to be involved in a reversal of the Nazi destruction, in a regaining of meaning which the Nazis had demolished.

The class therefore went through a process in which their easy assumptions and reassuring attitudes had to be destroyed before the students could rethink their identities. They had to become speechless with the terror of trauma before they could talk sensibly, or rather stammer, about it. As one student put it:

> Viewing the Holocaust testimony was for me initially catastrophic—so much of the historical coverage of it functions to empty it from its horror. Yet, in the week that followed the first screening, and throughout the remainder of the class, I felt increasingly implicated in the pain of the testimony, which found a particular reverberation in my own life …
>
> Literature has for me become the site of my own stammering. Literature, as that which can sensitively bear witness to the Holocaust, gives me a voice, a right, and a necessity to survive. Yet, I cannot discount the literature which in the dark awakens the screams, which opens the wounds, and which makes me want to fall silent. Caught by two contradictory wishes at once, to speak or not to speak, I can only stammer. Literature, for me, in these moments, has had a performative value: my life has suffered a burden, undergone a transference of

> pain. If I am to continue reading, I must, like David Copperfield, read *as if for life.* (Felman 1995: 58)

Felman's conclusion is that teachers of literature have the paradoxical task "of creating in the class the highest state of crisis that it [can] withstand, without 'driving the students crazy', without compromizing the students' bounds" (56). The teacher's duty is not only one of *transmitting*, but also of *accessing* the crisis which is inherent in the literary subjects.

> The question is, then, on the one hand, how to access, how *not to foreclose* the crisis, and, on the other hand, how to *contain it,* how much of the crisis the class can sustain.
>
> It is the teacher's task to recontextualize the crisis and to put it back into perspective, to relate the present to the past and to the future and to thus reintegrate the crisis in a *transformed* frame of meaning. (Felman 1995: 56)

Our conclusion is, in agreement with Felman, that readers should be guided by literary narratives to confront their own suppressed traumas and also become conscious of others' traumas—but only to the extent that they can bear it. We need sensitive, not shattered readers. We need to follow a middle way, between being unaware of suffering and being overwhelmed by it.

Understanding trauma?

Stories of trauma are often not understood, as Kathryn Robson explains:

> Survivors of trauma are only too frequently compelled to tell a story that is unacceptable, even unbelievable, within their social context because it breaks through the values shoring up the social contract. Survivors often face a double challenge: to put into words that which seems to resist narrativization and to recount experiences that cut through society's convictions. (Robson 2004: 12–13)

Narrators are generally supposed to tell coherent stories, to keep to the topic and make the point of the story clear—but traumatic stories defy these claims. Lise Schnell, an English professor whose daughter died at the age of two, tried to narrate the experience of losing her child, and came to the following conclusion:

> My students get tired of hearing me ask, over and over again, "What's the point, where is this essay headed?" Yet when it comes to my own project, and people ask me what the "thesis" is of my book, I have to say rather shamefacedly, that there really is none. There can be none. There is no coherent shape, no traceable

outline, in the encounter of life and death, just as there is hardly ever a coherence to life. (Schnell 2000: 29)

Traumatic experience, according to Cathy Caruth, is "a crisis that is marked, not by a simple knowledge, but by the ways it simultaneously defies and demands our witness" (Caruth 1996: 5). This crisis, which is partly a language crisis, has two sides to it: the problem for the traumatised person in narrating what has happened, in a language comprehensible for the non-traumatised; and the problem for the scholar in trying to understand and theorise about the survivors' narratives of trauma. Caruth believes that, because of the impenetrability of trauma, any language speaking about it will always be "somehow literary: a language that defies, even as it claims, our understanding" (5). This view is linked to the concept of a language of stammering, somewhere between silence and speaking, mentioned in a previous paragraph.

The basic paradox of writing about trauma, as we are doing here, is that it is about an experience which defies language; it is an experience suppressed into the subconscious because it is too overwhelming to be grasped. When the traumatic memory is turned into narrative, it is the beginning of a healing process, but it also means that the original experience is changed to fit into a narrative, so that its "real nature" still eludes our vision. It is impossible to comprehend the phenomenon of trauma—the utmost we can do, is attempt to assimilate a few of its many facets, and to gain fractions of meaning from the traumatic experience. Theorising about trauma has to start with the premise that the phenomenon studied resists all theorisation and defies an inclusive framework. And yet trauma cannot simply be ignored, since it takes such a central place in the personal and collective history of humanity; but the scholars of trauma should speak in a modest language, devoid of apodictic declarations.

The literary narrative, more than the academic language of scholars, is an appropriate medium for communication about trauma, as we have argued above. The modern novel often contains ambivalences, aporias and open endings; it lacks final certainties—and that makes it an extremely fitting vehicle for conveying the enigmatic experience of trauma. A huge trauma stimulates a response from authors, and a seemingly endless flow of literary narratives usually follows in its wake. There is never a final interpretation of any of these literary narratives—new readers continually find new meanings in them, and one and the same reader finds different meanings in the same narrative at different stages of her life. The story of literary narratives about trauma is a story with an open end.

The aim of traumatised people should not so much be to have finally grasped the trauma, but rather to make the continued grappling with it as rich in meaning as possible. For traumas, like traumatic stories, are never completely left behind; they too are never-ending. Traumatised people can be stimulated by the rich source of literary narratives to become creative artists in their own right, each one in her own way creating meaning out of chaos.

Charlotte Delbo: *Days and Memory*

Literary narratives can reveal more about trauma than abstract arguments can. Therefore we conclude this chapter with a discussion of a collection of literary narratives based on historical traumas: *Days and Memory* by Charlotte Delbo. The title of the original French version, which was published in 1985, two years after Delbo's death, is *La Mémoire et les Jours*. Delbo was working with a theatre group in South America when the Second World War broke out, and she returned to France to join her husband, Georges Dudach, in the resistance. They were caught by the French police; he was executed and she was held in prison for nine months before she was deported to Auschwitz in January 1943. After the war, she wrote extensively on her experiences in Auschwitz and other concentration camps; most famous is her trilogy, translated as *Auschwitz and After*.

Days and Memory has twenty-three chapters, containing rational argument, narratives, dialogues and poems—all of them focusing on the phenomenon of trauma. Some of the chapters are about what she herself experienced in Auschwitz, but there are also narratives about experiences of cruelty in Greece, Spain and the Soviet Union, pointing to the universality of the trauma experience. These events are all linked in her mind; they all form facets of the complex phenomenon of the trauma dominating her memory, which she wants to share with her readers. She uses different literary forms and genres in an attempt to respond adequately to the problem formulated in the first three words of the first chapter: "Explaining the inexplicable".

We mentioned Delbo's *Days and Memory* in chapter 1, referring to her explanation of the linguistic problem involved in talking about Auschwitz. The language itself is split in two. A word like "thirst", when used in everyday communication, refers to an experience radically different from what "thirst" meant in Auschwitz. Ordinary language proves insufficient to talk about extreme trauma. Delbo distinguishes between "intellectual" or "external" memory and "deep" memory. The former can be verbalised and narrated; the latter, the memory of severe trauma, resists formulation and narration, and is buried deep within the subconscious mind. Yet sometimes, in horrible nightmares, deep memory bursts into consciousness, with devastating effects.

In the first chapter of *Days and Memory*, Delbo uses the language of reasoning to explain the problem of talking about trauma—the fact that intellectual language is found lacking. In the following chapters, she uses typically literary ways of expression to translate deep memory into memory that can be verbalised and shared with others. This suggests a realisation that literary communication is more appropriate for the expression of trauma than the rational language used in her first chapter.

Yet even in the first chapter Delbo bases much of her argument on imagery, typical of literature—confirming what Caruth says, that writing and talking about trauma tends to use a language that is "somehow literary: a language that defies, even as it claims, our understanding" (Caruth 1996: 5). Thinking of her return from Auschwitz, Delbo says, "there comes to mind the image of a snake shedding its old skin, emerging from beneath it in a fresh, glistening one" (Delbo, 1990: 1). On her return, she maintains:

> I took leave of my skin—it had a bad smell, that skin—worn from all the blows it had received, and found myself in another, beautiful and clean, although with me the molting was not as rapid as the snake's. Along with the old skin went the visible traces of Auschwitz: the leaden stare out of sunken eyes, the tottering gait, the frightened gestures. With the new skin returned the gestures belonging to an earlier life … (Delbo, 1990:1)

The image used here, is a conventional one, suggesting that this traditional view of inner renewal fitted the Auschwitz experience. However, the image is soon turned upside down, and the snake skin becomes an image, not of renewal, but of a division between deep memory and intellectual memory. The snake has not really renewed itself; the past has not been left behind, but merely suppressed into the subconscious mind:

> It took a few years for the new skin to fully form, to consolidate. Rid of its own skin, it's still the same snake. I'm the same too, apparently. However …
>
> How does one rid oneself of something buried far within: memory and the skin of memory. It clings to me yet. Memory's skin has hardened, it allows nothing to filter out of what it retains, and I have no control over it. I don't feel it anymore. (Delbo, 1990: 1)

Instead of rescuing her, the skin is keeping part of her mind imprisoned; it prevents deep memory from entering consciousness and being worked through. Unable to recall deep memory at will, she has lost control over her past; she has become numb, not even able to feel the skin and its effects. Naively, one would think that the solution to this problem would be that the new skin should also be shed, like the previous one, to free the suppressed memory. Yet this skin, preventing her from working through suppressed memories and from integrating the subconscious mind with consciousness, also serves as a protection. When the skin is penetrated in nightmares so that deep memory enters the mind, the consequences are terrifying:

> In those dreams I see myself, yes, my own self such as I know I was: hardly able to stand on my feet, my throat tight, my heart beating wildly, frozen to the marrow, filthy, skin and bones; the suffering I feel is so unbearable, so identical to the pain endured there, that I feel it physically, I feel it throughout my whole body which becomes a mass of suffering: and I feel death fasten on me, I feel that I am dying. Luckily, in my agony I cry out. My cry wakes me and I emerge from the nightmare, drained. It takes days for everything to get back to normal, for everything to get shoved back inside memory, and for the skin of memory to mend again. I become myself again, the person you know, who can talk to you about Auschwitz without exhibiting or registering any anxiety or emotion. (Delbo, 1990: 3)

With her subversion of a conventional image of renewal, Delbo questions the belief in complete renewal. The image, as used by her, suggests the construction of an inner protection which makes it possible to continue living, but prevents her from dealing with the past—which helps her to survive but keeps her from healing. Indeed, it is a process which does not fit into conventional language or traditional views.

The analytical language of Delbo's first chapter changes into narrative language in the second. In this narrative, abstract ideas about trauma are embodied in the story about a specific character—a linking of the general with the specific which is impossible in the intellectual language used in the initial chapter. The "I" used by Delbo in the first chapter, changes into "she" as she tells about a woman who survived Auschwitz, but whose sister died there. With the use of the third person, Delbo becomes able to act as a witness to the suffering of other camp inmates, ensuring that their memory will survive—even if they are dead; even if nobody else relates their stories. Furthermore, the narrative is a way, for Delbo, of being released from the isolation of severe trauma that tends to encapsulate the sufferer with grief. Through the narrative, Delbo's personal suffering is included in a greater, collective suffering.

The story told in chapter 2 is another one containing a paradox that defies rational explanation. The woman who died in the camp is not really dead, since she continues living in her sister's memory—the surviving sister knew, "inside her she bore her sister, alive from now on through her alone" (Delbo, 1990: 6). The surviving sister, on the other hand, is not really alive, although she survived Auschwitz. She is overburdened by the past—"She came back home, but not back to life" (6). Her paradoxical state of being dead as well as alive is similar to that which Van Alphen noted in Holocaust testimonies, which we discussed above.

The intense emotion of the surviving woman is expressed by a rhythmical poetic prose in which key words, phrases and sounds are repeated:

> *Would she* be dead had the others not held her upright and got her to roll-call, *kept her* from falling into the ditch between the barracks and the mustering yard, *kept her* from fainting, *held her* on her feet till the end of the roll-call, *helped her* walk upon the icy road and reach the marsh, *would she* be dead? No. (Delbo, 1990: 5 – italics added.)

(Note that this analysis is based on the English translation for the benefit of English readers. It should be complemented by a study of the original French text, a study which is furthermore not limited to the first few chapters, as our discussion is.)

In this passage, the intense emotion contained in deep memory, is incorporated into the language of narrative, and the poetic language serves as a bridge between the subconscious and the conscious mind. The poetic prose of chapter 2 prepares the reader for the poem which forms the content of chapter 3. Here the strongly accentuated rhythm and the constant repetitions reveal an even more intense emotion.

> What is she holding in her arms
> hugged to her breast
> that one
> in the front row
> there, in the row facing ours
> yes that one in the front row.
> The ranks facing ours
> are still Gypsies.
> Yes, the Gypsies.
> How do you know it's a Gypsy when all that's left of it is a skeleton?
> Since the middle of the night they have been standing
> over there in the snow that thousands of feet have trampled into hardened slippery sheets
> Since the middle of the night
> we've been standing in the snow
> standing in the night
> the night broken by the spaced floodlights
> on the barbed wire fences

The motif of the barbed wire is repeated in the beginning of the following chapter: "The projectors light the barbed wire strung between high white poles" (9). The link indicates that these two chapters (3 and 4) are about the same episode in the camp: a policewoman trying in vain to pull a dead baby from a gypsy's arms, and then clubbing the gypsy mother to death. The poem expresses the intense emotion accompanying the narrative that is told in the following chapter; the phrases are like flashes of a nightmare emanating from deep memory.

Pronouns are skilfully alternated in chapter 4. “She” and “they” are mostly used when telling about the gypsies in the camp. However, this is complemented by the repeated use of “you” as well as “one” for the inmates of the camp, two words that seem to include the narrator in the group of onlookers. Indeed, once the narrator explicitly mentions her presence at the murder: “I look at the gypsy holding her baby pressed against her” (12). The alternation of third person pronouns with pronouns implying an all-encompassing generality (“one”, “you”, “each”) suggests a bond between the gypsy and all the witnesses of the event; and through the narrative the reader also becomes involved in this crowd of witnesses indicated by the “you” or “one”. Thus the narrative breaks through the bondage of trauma, which tends to isolate the traumatised in her suffering, as it creates a sister- and brotherhood of involved witnesses. Human empathy, which was destroyed in the Nazi camp, is revived.

The killing of the gypsy woman is told in a skilfully structured narrative. Not only is the alternation between the pronouns highly functional; the descriptions are extremely vivid, and the story holds the reader in suspense as it gradually moves to a climax. It is an illustration of what we stated above: that the chaos of trauma is transformed into order by the structure of an appropriate narrative.

This chapter started with the analysis of a dream narrative and concluded with an analysis of literary narratives based on historical trauma. In the following chapter, we will analyse a narrative that is completely fictional, yet is about traumatic experiences which are, especially for South Africans, close to the bone.

CHAPTER FIVE

WHEN THE ABSOLUTE FALLS INTO THE WATER …

J M Coetzee's *Disgrace*

In this chapter, we analyse *Disgrace* by J M Coetzee as an example of a text that portrays individual and communal traumas and suggests ways of healing. It is a book that deepens our understanding of ourselves and of the world we live in; that depicts various kinds of traumas and different possibilities of responding to them; that presents the reader with fundamental choices to be made. The novel brings together all the central themes of our book: life as a narrative; the search for meaning; trauma and the recreation of narratives; guilt, confession and forgiveness; and the role of ethical values in the healing of individuals and society. The concept of trauma is linked to the falling apart of a life story, to "losing the plot", to reaching a dead end road. Looking at *Disgrace* from this point of view, it is a work permeated by trauma. Although the narrative deals with the issues of contemporary South Africa, it has a much wider relevance, since South Africa is so clearly a microcosm of the world, containing the central problems, challenges and possibilities of the world at large.

Critical responses to *Disgrace*

There may be surprise at the choice of J M Coetzee's *Disgrace* to illustrate the healing possibilities of literary narratives. For many readers, it contained a disturbing rather than a healing narrative. Jany Poyner mentions some of the problems that South African readers have had with the novel:

> The metaphor of rape … is highly problematic in a country in which this crime is currently so prevalent, and which is reviled across the political spectrum. Coetzee chooses to write about African hooligans (skollies), the lowest element of black South African society, with whom Petrus—representative of legitimate black society—is in connivance. Black African agency is configured in the act of rape with devastating implications for a nation in which whites have regarded

> miscegenation with abhorrence and the black man as the natural rapist. (Poyner 2000: 71)

On the other hand, Poyner concedes that

> on a literary level, this portrayal tacitly accords with the terms of Sachs's proposition that art should be allowed to accommodate the most problematic facets of human existence—such a portrayal perhaps being made possible with the demise of apartheid. (Poyner 2000: 71) (For the reference to Sachs, see Sachs 1998.)

Many readers of the novel, especially South African ones, were disturbed by ideological overtones they thought they detected in it. To them, *Disgrace* opened old wounds instead of healing them; it constituted a step backwards from the New into the Old South Africa. Let us have a closer look at some of these ideological critics of *Disgrace.*

In the ANC's submission to the Human Rights Commission in 2000, presented by Public Enterprises Minister Jeff Radebe, the following was maintained about *Disgrace*:

> JM Coetzee represents as brutally as he can, the white people's perception of the post-apartheid black man … It is suggested that in these circumstances, it might be better that our white compatriots should emigrate because to be in post-apartheid South Africa is to be in "their territory", as a consequence of which the whites will lose their cars, their weapons, their property, their rights, their dignity. The white women will have to sleep with the barbaric black men. (ANC 2000)

The editor of the Afrikaans Sunday newspaper *Rapport*, Tim du Plessis, mentioned to the *New York Times*, at the time of the announcement of Coetzee's winning the Nobel Prize, that some people thought the renowned author was sending to the world a negative message about the new South Africa (quoted in Iannone 2005: 2). This reservation is linked to that of the ANC in that both criticise the perceived negative portrayal of the country and its people.

Annie Gagiano voiced a number of ideological reservations about Coetzee's writing, including *Disgrace* (Gagiano 2004). At the heart of her criticism is

> the persistent omission from Coetzee's texts of fully rounded and intellectually respected African characters … Coetzee's portrayal does little to counter and much to confirm the notorious "white funk" attitude and its foundation in a conviction that the advent of "black" power in South Africa means a "reversion to primitivity" (Gagiano 2004:42)

She perceives in Coetzee's work a "blindness to African incarnations of humanity, genius, and art" (46).

Gagiano is especially critical of the portrayal of the youngest of the rapists:

> How many readers, I wonder, will be able to resist the pattern of dehumanising descriptions of this 'child', given his participation in a heinous deed, and how many (especially 'white' South African readers) will not be inclined to associate Coetzee's account of this young man with the litanies of rape and molestation in our newspapers? Has the novel deepened our sense of underlying causes, or has in instead foregrounded one of the more glaringly 'spectacular' and 'racially' polarising aspects of South African society? (Gagiano 2004: 43)

Harsh criticism was also levelled against *Disgrace* in an article by Beverley Roos Muller in the *Weekend Argus* of 22 January 2000 (Magazine section p 20). We quote some of the relevant statements:

> David Lurie … appears to not only be incapable of having any mature relationships with women, but more significantly, to be incapable of seeing them as fully co-human. His two divorces, his use and abuse of sex workers, his dysfunctional daughter, portrayed as a lumpy lesbian, and his hunting of a vulnerable student, is not only apologized for, but condoned as having enriched his life: "like a flower blooming in his breast, his heart floods with thankfulness"…
>
> [The book] carries a moral weight which is without hope, without the possibility of redemption …
>
> Coetzee's portrayal of the daughter's dilemma (a young woman he portrays particularly unsympathetically) goes beyond the bounds of credibility: her reaction to violence, to rape, to the destruction of her chosen environment and those creatures in her care, with a kind of passive fatalism …
>
> The only thing more reprehensible than inadequate or imperfect ethical behaviour is the contempt of the attempt …
>
> Is Coetzee feeding off (or worse, feeding up) the national paranoia?
>
> Coetzee's story … offers no possibility of Grace.

In the following analysis, it will become clear in which ways our reading of the novel differs from that of the above-mentioned readers. However, we would like to make a few remarks at the outset. It is vitally important that a distinction should be made between the main character and the implied author, that is, between the opinions of the David Lurie and the world view implied in the book. There are indications that the implied author often dissociates himself from Lurie's views and deeds. One cannot, as Roos does, blame the author for the flaws of his fictional character—the book gives an honest portrayal of the main character without condoning all his actions. It is also important to note that

Lurie changes in the course of the narrative—one should distinguish the early Lurie from the later one. David gradually develops a sense of ethics, though he often does not have the inner strength to act accordingly. The novel portrays human failings highlighted within the context of ethical ideals.

Gagiano is irritated by "the litanies of rape and molestation in our newspapers"; she prefers to hear less bad news about the new South Africa and also wants Coetzee to focus more on the positive aspects of the country and its people. This is an understandable argument; but it is overshadowed by the fact that, for the healing of the country to take place, the remaining wounds have to be brought to light. Coetzee should not necessarily be blamed for the harsh portrayal of aspects of the country—it could be seen as an honest depiction of tensions still existing in the community.

> While the legacy of non-racialism … has infiltrated the contemporary in policy formulations, in the minds of a new generation of South Africans it exists by and large in uneven, dissipated fragments. The desired world of non-racialism, while having been sighted and given the nod, still remains a fiction. (Viljoen 2001: 52)

The portrayal of the black characters in particular was worrying to the ANC and to Gagiano. However, one cannot generalise about the portrayal of black people on the basis of the few black characters in the book. The rapists represent an element that does exist in the black (and white) community, but it would be absurd to see them as representative of black characters in general. Granted, the black characters in the novel are involved in the rape of a white woman—but placed in the context of the novel, and, more importantly, in the context of South African history, the actions of the rapists and of the foreman Petrus (who seems to be behind the rape) become more understandable—though not permissible. One should also remember that David's own deeds often resemble those of a rapist, so that the black men's rape of Lucy is balanced by "rapes" committed by David. There is no trace of "'European' superiority and 'African' inferiority'" (Gagiano 2004: 47) in the book; on the contrary, Western history, even the English language, is laden with guilt. The novel gives a harsh portrayal, not of Africans, but of men; a portrayal that is balanced by a sympathetic, admiring depiction of the central female characters, Lucy and Bev. If there is a dividing line in the novel, it is between males and females, not between black and white. In the following pages, this argument will be developed more fully.

Gagiano is extremely critical of Coetzee's portrayal of the youngest rapist. Although she acknowledges that one should remember that "the person describing him is Lurie, father of the gang rape victim" (43), she totally underplays David's subjectivity in her criticism of the representation of the rapist. The fact that this young man is so repulsive to David, makes Lucy's compassion towards him so much more remarkable; it highlights the contrast between father and daughter. Lucy's attitude to the young man clearly indicates that there are alternative, more ethical, ways of reacting to him than those of her father. To expect the author not to portray a rapist as he is perceived by the rapist's father, because of the associations that may be evoked in "many (especially 'white' South African readers)" (43), is to severely limit the creativity of the artist.

Perhaps the most sensitive issue for South African readers touched upon in *Disgrace* is the rape of a white woman by a black man. This is partly what Roos Muller had in mind when she talks about "feeding off (or worse, feeding up) the national paranoia". The fact that the rape of a white woman by black men is accepted by the woman as punishment for "the sins of the fathers", and that she is clearly admired by the implied author for her attitude—all this is more than many readers could stomach. However, one should remember that rape is not portrayed as something acceptable in the novel—Lucy did not invite rape, it happened, and then she had to work through it. In her working through it, the rape does not become less horrible, but rather more meaningful. Her ultimate response is not acquiescence to rape but, on the contrary, a sacrifice in order to make an end to raping.

It is also important to mention the deliberate silences of the novel here. The silences in the telling of the rape as well as in the portrayal of Petrus are striking. Lucy Valerie Graham sounds a note of warning about the elision of the details of Lucy's rape in the novel, saying that "to consign rape to a space outside articulation may contribute to a wider phenomenon of silencing" (Graham 2003: 444). However, one should remember that this silence is part of a pattern of suggestions about the limitations of David Lurie's perspective—there are many things that Lurie does not know and cannot understand, and therefore he keeps quiet about them. It is in any case debatable whether something as terrible as a rape can be communicated adequately through language; but it is certain that Lucy would never tell her father exactly what happened, for he would clearly not understand. (In contrast, Lucy apparently tells her friend Bev in detail about what happened.) So David maintains a silence about matters that are beyond his knowledge and understanding.

Gagiano does not take the important theme of "silences" sufficiently into account. She bemoans the fact that the novel does not contain rounded, intelligent African characters. The point of the novel is that David is unable to understand or to tell the story of African characters properly—the novel deals with the abyss between them. As far as the portrayal of Petrus is concerned, it is suggested that he may have an interesting life story to tell, but it is outside the scope of David's knowledge and imagination. The implied author deliberately limits himself, throughout the narrative, to the perspective of his male main character, thereby implying his own limited knowledge and limited ability to narrate. The novel could be read as an "invitation" for other narrators to recount from their experience what is here deliberately omitted.

Roos Muller levels sharp criticism at the novel's perceived lack of ethics, its failure to offer possibilities for redemption or grace. Later on we will analyse the ethical content of the novel extensively, its suggestions of redemption and grace. At this point, we merely want to note our agreement with some insightful remarks by Mike Marais:

> What one finds in this novel is therefore a depiction of a society that is characterized by a denial of otherness, that is, by an absence of ethics. At the same time, the novel self-consciously describes the ethical possibilities of literary writing in such a totalising context. Since writing establishes a unique relation to alterity, it is able to expose both writer and reader to that which they routinely deny and whose denial enables violence …
>
> Levinas … maintains that the exposure of the autonomous subject to the other forestalls violence by rendering the subject responsible for the other. Importantly, responsibility here is not a modality of sympathy but of the *substitution* of self with the other. Instead of affirming itself by foreclosing on the other, the self *gives* itself to the other and this gift takes the form of a sacrifice. (Marais 2000: 62)

In *Disgrace,* Marais suggests, the reader is confronted by a lack of ethical behaviour in the society depicted and by the violence resulting from it. This lack of harmony stimulates the reader to look for ethical alternatives where people open themselves up to others, where one person takes responsibility for another. The most striking example of ethical behaviour in the novel is presented by Lucy who, instead of affirming herself, gives herself and makes a sacrifice that offers hope of an end to the continuing violence.

Although we cannot hope to convince all readers of all aspects of our interpretation of the novel, it is important to focus on the issues where we believe agreement to be possible. We hope that the novel's treatment of ethics is a point where divergent opinions may converge. This is also the central point in our argument, because we believe that the road to healing is inevitably an ethical one. Although it is true, as many critics have remarked, that *Disgrace* focuses on 'European' characters while the African characters remain on the periphery, the narrative touches on ethical themes where the significance of the distinction between Europe and Africa fades away, for these themes have a relevance to all.

After this brief response to some of the views expressed on the ethics and ideology of *Disgrace*, it is now necessary to offer our own analysis of the book from the perspective of narrative as a means of making meaning of trauma. (For a further discussion of South African responses to the novel, see Derek Attridge's Introduction in Attridge & McDonald (2002), as well as the articles "*Race in Disgrace*" by David Attwell, and "*Disgrace Effects*" by Peter McDonald, in the same volume (2002: 315–320, 331–341, 321–330).)

David Lurie's dead end roads

David Lurie, the main character, reaches a number of dead end roads in the course of the story. He is a failure in his relationship with women. Married twice and divorced twice, his narrative is not one that could contain the familiar words: "And then they got married and lived happily ever after." After his divorces David became a womaniser, and "for decades, that was the backbone of his life" (Coetzee 1999: 7); but this way of living stopped abruptly when he got too old to be attractive to women.

The next step is the establishment of a relationship with the attractive prostitute Soraya, whom he visits regularly once a week. To David it is a substitute marriage, one that fulfils his sexual desires without demanding any responsibilities from him "the morning after" (2). She provides his rather miserable life with purpose and joy—in the "desert" of the week, his visit to her becomes an oasis (1). The relationship is based on illusion, however, because Soraya does not belong to him—she has a life of her own, with a husband and children; and when David happens to meet her and her family in town, the illusion is shattered. In her life story, David is on the margin, and his only role there is a financial one. After this meeting Soraya refuses to keep on seeing him once a week, but David does not want to acknowledge defeat. Life has now become "as featureless as a desert" (11), and he desperately tries to resume contact with Soraya. He harasses her and becomes a "rapist" in the sense that he tries to force his will upon her and invade her story. His attempts are unsuccessful, however, and the relationship leads to another dead end for David.

If rape is characterised by sexual gratification combined with the abuse of power, then David is even more of a rapist in his next sexual relationship. His attractive student Melanie is clearly not interested in his advances, and when he takes her out for a meal in Hout Bay, she "stares out glumly over the sea" (19). Afterwards, when he makes love to her, she does not refuse him but "is passive throughout" (19). The self-centred David does not care how she feels about him; he is delighted that his sexual desires have been gratified by a beautiful young woman, and "he wakes the next morning in a state of profound wellbeing" (19). In a subsequent encounter, when Melanie tries to resist him, he ignores her resistance and overpowers her: "Nothing will stop him. He carries her to the bedroom" (25). This intercourse is essentially a rape, and afterwards David feels the need, for himself as well as for Melanie, to be cleansed by bathing.

In more than one respect the relationship with Melanie is a relationship between the powerful and the powerless: the male overpowers the female, the professor the student, and—probably—the white man the "coloured". There are a number of suggestions that Melanie is not white. David thinks of her as "Meláni: the dark one" (18), with the name suggesting that she is melanic, that is, dark in pigmentation. As an actress, she plays the role of a "coloured" character with a glaring *Kaapse*[7] accent (24), and the unattractive school where her father is principal, looks like a school for "coloureds" rather than whites (164). In his relationship with Melanie, David is in a way continuing the old colonial discourse of subjection, and, typical of his life story, he loses the person whom he wants to possess and dominate.

When David's behaviour towards Melanie is investigated by a university committee, his response to the charges is full of contradictions. He admits being guilty, offers no excuses, but also shows no remorse. For him, "repentance belongs to another world, another universe of discourse" (58), and he is clearly not interested in entering that universe. His daughter Lucy later on calls him, half jokingly, a "moral dinosaur" (89), and, in a moral sense, his views are indeed primeval. He justifies, to Lucy, his behaviour as "the rights of desire" (89), but is unable to admit the equal rights of other people's desires. His blind narcissism is rationalised in language with a religious flavour: "My case rests … on the god who makes even the small birds quiver" (89). This god upon whom he calls to strengthen his case, is a terrifying one who makes powerless little birds tremble—David is projecting his own lust for power onto the god whom he honours.

The loss of Melanie leads to another loss for David—the loss of his job. In a way, he had lost his job before the charge brought by Melanie led to his resignation. The former "Cape Town University College" has been turned into the "Cape Technical University" (3); the focus is now on practical communication, and David becomes a teacher of Communications. He finds the first premise of the Communications course that he has to teach, objectionable: that language originated in the desire to communicate. For David, "the origins of speech lie in song, and the origins of song in the need to fill out with sound the overlarge and rather empty human soul" (4). In this environment, there is no room for a study of language and literature to fill the emptiness of his soul. The Technical University does allow him to offer one course that interests him, namely on the Romantic poets, but here the ignorance of the students is staggering: "post-Christian, posthistorical, postliterate, they might as well have been hatched from eggs yesterday" (32).

---

[7] Literally "Cape", implying Cape Town and nearby.

No woman, no job, no language study to fill his empty soul; he decides to visit his daughter Lucy at the distant village of Salem, hoping to find peace there. In her hospitality, in her willingness to allow him a part in her meaningful existence, he hopes to find a "second salvation" (86). But then, once more, his hope is shattered and his life story reaches a dead end. Lucy is raped by three black men, and David, who is unable to protect her, is beaten and burnt. This event leads to a number of other events shocking for David: Lucy's loss of the ownership of her land (for which David has partly paid); Lucy's falling pregnant from the rape; her decision not to have an abortion; and her decision to accept the offer of Petrus, the former labourer on her small-holding, to marry her. For somebody still belonging, in his heart of hearts, to the old South Africa, David's world must have fallen apart. His grandchild would be the child of an unknown rapist; his son-in-law would be a black man, previously Lucy's labourer, who already has two other (black) wives.

The different reactions of David and Lucy to the rape lead to the parting of their ways. David refuses to relinquish his old role towards his daughter, that of the dominating father. In so many ways, he "has become a refuge for old thoughts" (72). Lucy's reaction to his attitude is significant:

> You behave as if everything I do is part of the story of your life. You are the main character, I am a minor character … I am not a minor. I have a life of my own, just as important to me as yours is to you, and in my life I am the one who makes the decisions. (198)

If the essence of rape lies in subjection, in violating others' life stories, then David is essentially a rapist of his daughter, as he was of his student Melanie.

New developments in David's narrative

The total loss of meaning in every aspect of his life initially leads David to a deep despair:

> The blood of life is leaving his body and despair is taking its place, despair that is like a gas, odourless, tasteless, without nourishment. You breathe it in, your limbs relax, you cease to care, even at the moment when the steel touches your throat. (Coetzee 1999: 108)

Then developments take place that lead to a gradual return of life to his empty soul. David enters a "universe of discourse" (58) for which he previously had only contempt, a universe where repentance belongs: the universe of ethical thinking and behaviour. Ethical discourse is based on the ability to put oneself in another's shoes, to balance one's own needs and desires with those of others, and to look at oneself from somebody else's perspective—especially somebody one has wronged. Without this ability no repentance is possible for the perpetrator.

The rape of Lucy helps David to look anew at what he did to Melanie. If, through the abuse of power, David had in reality raped his student, then the tables have now been turned, with his daughter at the receiving end of a rape and both of them experiencing the fate of the powerless. This great trauma helps David to look at his own deeds from a different angle and stimulates new feelings and actions. The fact that he could not protect his daughter causes him feelings of guilt and shame (157)—emotions conspicuously absent when he was questioned by the university committee. He decides to visit Melanie's home, which means that he will be entering her family network and confronting the damage that he caused there. The visit leads to surprising events: David asks Mr Isaacs, Melanie's father, for his pardon, and bows before Melanie's mother and sister, humbling himself and acknowledging his guilt. David has left his narcissistic prison and is entering an ethical sphere.

Through his contact with Lucy and her friend, Bev Shaw, David learns that animals too must be included in the realm of ethics. Lucy tells him sharply:

> This is the only life there is. Which we share with the animals. That's the example that people like Bev try to set. That's the example I try to follow. To share some of our human privilege with the beasts. I don't want to come back in another existence as a dog or a pig and have to live as dogs or pigs live under us. (75)

There seems to be a contradiction between Lucy's emphatic belief in this life as the only one, and her mentioning another existence where she may be reincarnated as an animal. Be that as it may, the important point here is that Lucy makes no moral distinction between people and animals. Bev, whose example Lucy tries to follow, talks to animals as if they were people: "What do you say, my friend?" she whispers to a goat in her clinic, and after the session she comments on the animal: "Such a good old fellow, so brave and straight and confident" (83). At the end of the novel, David describes the "soft, short smell of the released soul" in the room where the animals die (219). To him, there is no more doubt that animals have souls too.

David offers to help Bev in her clinic, and gradually grows attached to the animals under her care. Sue Kossew notes:

> Despite David's resolution not to change, it is the dogs that unleash his emotions—'the more killings he assists in, the more jittery he gets' (142). He cries and "does not understand what is happening to him" as his indifference towards animals dissipates from an "abstract" disapproval of cruelty to a personal

> commitment to the dogs and, through them, to "his idea of the world" (146). In "offering himself to the service of dead dogs", the "selfish" David finds a kind of grace for himself and the dogs, a way of working through the endlessness of his skepticism and towards repentance. (Kossew 2003: 160)

The dogs provide his life with a new meaning and purpose; he feels a moral obligation towards them and confesses betrayal when he leaves them temporarily (78). The clinic ultimately becomes a home (211) that takes the place of his previous abode, which is no home to him any longer. He identifies with the "disgrace" of the animals' dying and helps them to die in a dignified way. Especially one dog, one that likes the music he composed, earns his affection. Here the distinction between man and dog completely fades away, because David is also a lonely "old dog" who has to face the disgrace of dying; the dog is almost an alter ego of David. Feeling at home with the dogs, he is learning to feel "at home" with himself; loving and caring for the dogs, he is learning to love and care for himself.

Much more than his involvement with the animals, David's creative work brings meaning to his life and drives out his despair. Composing an opera fascinates him, touches him to the core (214). At last he has found something that fills his empty soul (4), a way of triumphing over the triviality and transience of his life. His opera *Byron in Italy* gives a new "lease of life" to the deceased characters on which his work is based—Byron and his mistress Teresa—for their memory will be preserved in a work of art; but they, in their turn, provide him with a voice that can last when he has died. He transforms his own banal feelings into something beautiful; he projects his transitory experiences into something timeless and true, an opera with an "authentic note of immortal longing" (214). David's opera contains the fundamental aspects of his humanity: moral shortcomings, passionate longing and love—all cast in a comical, ironic vein, called forth by the tones of a banjo (184). In writing an opera about Byron and Teresa, David is also rewriting his own identity, for, in inventing the opera, he is inventing himself (186), discovering and expressing the essential, suppressed aspects of his life.

Through projecting essential aspects of himself and his life onto the various characters in the opera, David has discovered an indirect way of expressing himself: like Byron, he is lascivious, a Romantic, and an exile; like Byron's mistress Teresa, he has an immortal longing. In the opera, Teresa, like Lucy, can love more strongly than her male pendant, and is able to make greater sacrifices. Teresa succeeds, through her steadfast love, in bringing her beloved Byron back from the underworld; similarly, in his own life, Lucy in her steadfastness becomes a moral guide to David and helps him not disintegrate completely. David, who cannot really communicate with other people, discovers in his creative work a way of healing through indirect self-expression.

David is in fact practising Viktor Frankl's logotherapy by creating a story that gives meaning to his life. What started as fragments (141), has been turned into something coherent and meaningful. Note, however, that "logotherapy" is here practised from the writer's point of view, not from the reader's, as discussed in chapters 1 and 3. Note too, that David is still in control when writing his opera—this is the only kind of relationship of which he is capable. He has never been able to have a sound human relationship where his story merges with another's; but in his opera he can create a story without outside interference; he must love only the characters that he himself has created (182). Even at the end of the novel, when he becomes very fond of a particular dog, it is still David who is in control—he is the one to decide when the dog should die. Although David does change in a positive way during the narrative, he is only able to take a few small steps. He is not a heroic character, but rather pathetic, and the banjo is the right instrument to express, indirectly, the comical and ironic tone of the composer's life.

Contrasting discourses

Disgrace is not only about David's individual traumas and his ways of working through them; it also deals with the collective trauma of a divided society. It was mentioned in the first chapter of this book that the inhabitants of a country "imagine a community", they transform the data about the past into a story that provides them with an identity and a vision of the past, present and future. In 1994, a "New South Africa" was formed, free from the apartheid laws of the past; but many of the old dividing lines still remained, as is indicated in *Disgrace*. Not much of a "rainbow nation"—the metaphor coined by Archbishop Tutu—is to be seen in Coetzee's novel. It is quite clear that David and the black characters (Petrus and the rapists) are situated in two radically opposed political discourses, two different communal stories about South Africa. Petrus's discourse is the new one emerging in South Africa, a discourse linked to black people's coming into power and being able to tell their own story about the country—not the story of their previous masters. David's communal story, on the other hand, still belongs to the old South Africa.

Oppression by colonialists is at the heart of the South African story believed by Petrus and the rapists. Subjugation by the colonists, as experienced by the indigenous people, is linked to the central theme of rape in the novel. The rapists feel that their raping is justified, because it balances the "rape" of colonialism. As David correctly points out: "It was history speaking through them … A history of wrong … It may have seemed personal, but it wasn't. It came down from the ancestors" (156).

The difference in discourse leads to the diametrically opposite views of David and Petrus about right and wrong. To David the rape of Lucy was a terrible crime against his innocent daughter and he wants justice, his view of justice, to be done—the criminals must be brought before a court and receive the sentence that they deserve. For Petrus, on the other hand, the injustices of the past have been balanced out by Lucy's rape. Therefore he maintains that, after the rape, "it is all right" (138)—justice has been restored, Lucy has paid for the sins of the ancestors. To him, it was a rape to end rapes.

Nowhere is the vast abyss between the worlds of David and Petrus shown more clearly than at the beginning of chapter 9. David is watching a soccer match on television, with the commentary alternating between Sotho and Xhosa. He is not much interested in the game and does not understand the languages anyway, so it is no surprise that he falls asleep. When he wakes up, Petrus is beside him, he has turned up the volume and is full of enthusiasm for the game, since the Bushbuck soccer team is one of his favourites. When the game is over, Petrus switches the channel to boxing, so David decides to leave the television room. This scene is told without narrative commentary, but the point is clear: to David, Petrus is a stranger with a different language and an alien culture.

Yet David acknowledges that Petrus probably also has an interesting story, and he would not mind hearing it (117). That story, however, cannot be told in English: "More and more he is convinced that English is an unfit medium for the truth of South Africa … Pressed into the mould of English, Petrus's story would come out arthritic, bygone" (117). Two points about English are relevant here. It is obvious that Petrus could not tell his story in a language that would not fit the content, and in which he is not proficient; he would need his mother tongue to tell the story of his life and his people. The narratives of South Africa need to be told in a variety of languages. The second point made about English is that the sins of colonialism have contaminated it. When Petrus uses the word "benefactor" to describe Lucy, it is to David a distasteful word with patronising associations. David concludes:

> The language he [Petrus] draws on with such aplomb is, if he only knew it, tired, friable, eaten from the inside as if by termites … Nothing short of starting all over again with the ABC. (129)

David uses English as a fit medium for the opera he writes about Byron, but knows that it is not appropriate for the story of Petrus. The absence of the latter story is one of the deliberate silences in the novel, suggesting that David's knowledge and understanding are lacking, and his language is insufficient to tell what needs to be told.

It is extremely important to remember the perspective from which the story of *Disgrace* is told. An external narrator is used, which lends the story an aura of objectivity and trustworthiness. Yet it must be remembered that the whole world of the novel is seen from David's perspective; therefore the reader receives no more information about the other characters than that which David observes and relates. *Disgrace* is not so much about the new South Africa as about a disillusioned white male's experience of the new South Africa. David's views are not presented as totally reliable, nor his character as flawless—on the contrary. Other ways of life, other possible responses to the situation are depicted beside those of David—we find the "polyphony of voices" mentioned in chapter 4. Bev and Lucy are most relevant here. It is clear that David comes to admire both of them. Towards the end of the novel, when the conclusions of the narrative begin to crystallise, David expresses his admiration for Lucy (216, 218). Bev and Lucy—especially Lucy—embody the ideals that David appreciates but is unable to realise in his own life. *Disgrace* does not purport to contain "the whole truth about the new South Africa", but rather the truth about a white male struggling to adapt to new conditions.

The desires of Petrus

There are suggestions in the novel that Petrus, the man whose story David does not tell, is an interesting man, a man with a story, well worth some attention. Initially he is "the gardener and the dog-man" (64), employed by Lucy. Gradually their roles are reversed. For Petrus, black power in South Africa must lead to black ownership of the land; more specifically, he should become the owner of Lucy's land. He goes about in a shrewd and relentless way to get what he wants. During the time that Lucy is raped, Petrus is conspicuously absent, but later one of the rapists attends the feast that Petrus organises. It is clear that Petrus knows about the rape and has probably organised it to get Lucy out of the way.

Petrus is a practical man, doing what needs to be done to let the new era materialise. His activities on the market are symbolic of the role he eventually plays in the handing over of power: "Petrus is the one who swiftly and efficiently lays out their wares, the one who knows the prices, takes the money, makes the change … Petrus does what needs to be done, and that is that" (116). In a similar way, he organises a deal with Lucy—as Lucy puts it: "He is offering an alliance, a deal. I contribute the land, in return for which I am allowed to creep in under his wing" (203). Petrus is negotiating a deal which is fair in his eyes: Lucy has paid a sufficient price for staying on the farm under his protection; his claim on ownership of the land is based on historical injustice, on Europeans having taken the land from the Africans. To him, a just deal has been concluded. Linked to the above symbolism is the cleaning of the dam by Petrus and David. This scene follows after David has been thinking about Petrus's desire to take over Lucy's land (117–118). The cleaning of the dam points symbolically to the cleaning up the mess of history—so that Petrus can get the share which he has been denied. It should be noted that Petrus takes the lead here; David helps him for a while, and then stops. The roles of "baas en Klaas"[8] (116) have been turned around.

Petrus is the one who knows first when the new era has truly begun on the farm, and he organises a feast to celebrate, inviting Lucy and David to it—he feels magnanimous towards them, allows them a part in the festivities. Two sheep are slaughtered for the feast—symbolically, Lucy and David are the two sheep that have to suffer for the sake of the dawning of the new age. No wonder David feels a bond between him and the two sheep (126), just as he later on develops a bond with the dying dogs. At this ritual feast, confirming that the new times have come, the contrasting responses of David and Lucy to the changed situation become clear. When one of the rapists turns up, David wants to have him arrested, whereas Lucy wants to lay the matter to rest. Symbolically, Lucy accepts her role as the sacrificial lamb, David rebels against it.

Petrus's name suggests that he is reliable as a rock. He is not reliable in the way that David and the old farmer Ettinger expect him to be (109): that he should do what they demand and protect them against danger. However, when Petrus has had his way in the dealings, it is suggested that he will indeed be a protecting rock for Lucy (138). In his own way, he is a solid character, certain of his goals and unflinching in realising them. Yet he is not without blemish. His desire to have the land is almost like a sexual desire, the kind of desire that earlier led David to "take possession of" Melanie.

Petrus is clearly one who likes possessions; at the end of the novel he owns Lucy's land and also "possesses" three wives, Lucy included. The root cause of the injustices of the past, namely the insatiable desire to overpower and possess, is present also in Petrus, so that the new era carries seeds of destruction similar to those in the previous one. It is suggested that a new patriarchy is at hand under the rule of Petrus, the man who condoned the rape of a woman. One of Petrus's wives is pregnant, and he prays that she will have a boy rather than a girl, because a boy can show his sisters how to behave—the men are clearly calling the tune in his household. The highest compliment he can pay Lucy, is that she is (almost) "as good as a boy" (130).

---

[8] Master and servant.

Counteracting the hate and violence: Lucy's sacrifice

Lucy is caught up between two male characters, her father and her labourer. They have different life stories and conflicting desires; reconciliation and peace between them seem to be unattainable. In the first story, Lucy's land lawfully belongs to her, in the other, justice demands that it be returned to Petrus; in the one, the rape was a crime, in the other, the restoration of justice. Both David and Petrus are dominating males with a lack of consideration for women. The situation is exacerbated by Petrus's collaborators, the rapists, with their hate that struck Lucy so forcefully: "It was so personal … It was done with such personal hatred" (156). The humanity of the rapists has been narrowed down to one overwhelming emotion, namely hate towards white people. Their hate allows no room for compassion, for ethical considerations, for looking at their actions from the victim's perspective. All these male characters surrounding Lucy are, to a greater or lesser extent, caught up in their own narrow discourses.

For Lucy there is only one way to end the violent conflicts and earn the right to stay on the farm, but it is not an easy way. Lucy does not tell her father anything about what happened, to "get it off her chest", because she realises that he would not understand her way of thinking and would not support her course of action. She is a strong woman, able to face her situation, think it through independently and act according to her conclusions. Yet, before she sees the light, Lucy goes through a sombre period where she "spends hour after hour lying on her bed, staring into space or looking at old magazines" (114). Then she decides to accept the reality of the new discourse of power, as administered by Petrus, and become part of it. This demands a set of sacrifices from her: she leaves the discourse where she is the innocent victim of a rape attack and enters a story where she will be identified with the rapists. In this story, justice requires that she should give up her claim to the land and become one of Petrus's wives. Her self-sacrifice is the opposite of rape; whereas rape is an act of taking possession, sacrifice is one of letting go; rape is an act of subjection, sacrifice one of submission. Thus her action is an antidote to the rape permeating the world around her. In her decision, Lucy is not led by abstractions such as guilt and salvation (112), but rather by the concrete needs of the situation. Having decided that she wants to stay on the land, she does what needs to be done to realise this goal.

Lucy is determined to counteract the hate around her by love and forgiveness; she realises that the cycle of violence will continue and intensify as long as violence is returned in kind. Here the contrast between father and daughter is clear. David is enraged when he sees one of the rapists, a mentally unbalanced young boy, staring at Lucy, half-dressed, through her bedroom window. This time, David, wanting the boy to be at the receiving end of savage behaviour, kicks him and hits him and allows his dog to finish the job. When Lucy comes on to the scene, she pulls the dog from the boy, enquires about his condition and washes his wounds—even though the boy shouts, "We will kill you all!" (207). Lucy is not so embittered that she cannot recognise that the boy is "a disturbed child" (208) and that one cannot expect "normal" behaviour from him. She also realises that the boy is part of the reality of the farm life that she has chosen and cannot be wished away. David, on the other hand, although he admits the boy's abnormality (207), expects "civilised" behaviour from him—David is acting instinctively, like a "moral dinosaur". Lucy's determination to conquer hate with love is also seen in her decision not to abort the child she is expecting from a rapist. She refuses to project the hate of the child's father towards her onto the baby; the violence of the father is countered by her love towards his child (216). Into the dark world of violence and hate around her, Lucy shines the light of loving kindness suggested by her name (Lucy comes from the Latin "lux", meaning "light").

The fact that Lucy is lesbian, is part of her "statement of independence" (89), part of the creation of her own life story, free from the demands of the community. Through this she escapes from the conventional binary opposition of male and female. On the one hand, she conforms to roles traditionally associated with women: women are good at cleaning up the mess; women are more forgiving than men (69); women are used to sacrificing themselves. On the other hand, Lucy takes roles traditionally assigned to men: farming, negotiating, pioneering. In portraying Lucy as a female farmer giving up her land, Coetzee is writing in direct opposition to the conventions of the traditional farm novel (*plaasroman*), a genre that was the theme of two of Coetzee's essays (Coetzee 1988: 63–81 (*Farm Novel and Plaasroman*) and 82–114 (*The Farm Novels of C M van den Heever*)). As is typical in the conventional farm novel, Lurie leaves the detestable city to be saved on a farm—but the saving is totally different from the standard "farm novel" cure. In conventional farm novels, the farm almost always belongs to the Afrikaner male; but here the owner of the land is English, female, and a lesbian to boot. Traditionally, it was sacrilege for the farmer to give up the farm; a mystic bond was perceived to exist between farmer and farm, a bond which had to be handed from father to son. Lucy, in contrast, has no link with forebears from whom she inherited the land or with descendants who should inherit it from her. Her heroism does not exist in holding on to the farm at all costs, as in traditional *plaasromans*, but in giving it up. Her action in *Disgrace* cancels a long history of narratives in which men clung to the land. In its portrayal of the black labourer, *Disgrace* also radically deviates from conventional farm novels:

> Silence about the place of black labour … is common not only to Schreiner and Smith but, by and large, to the Afrikaans *plaasroman*, and represents a failure of

> imagination before the problem of how to integrate the dispossessed black man into the idyll. (Coetzee 1988: 71–72 (*Farm Novel and Plaasroman*))

By contrast, in *Disgrace* the black man reclaims the land and the old idyll is replaced by a realistic negotiation between black and white about power relations.

Disgrace is a novel about the divisions and wounds of South African society, but is also about ways of healing. As mentioned before, the novel contains a polyphony of voices. Readers can identify to different degrees with the various characters (the shock and anger of David at the rape of his daughter; his feelings of alienation in a changed country; Petrus's demand that the injustices of history be rectified; Bev's care for maltreated animals; Lucy's ability to adapt and sacrifice, etc.) as a way of confronting and refiguring their own life stories. Lucy, in collaboration with Petrus, creates a model of reconciliation on the farm that is relevant to the whole of South Africa and to the world at large. The novel allows the reader space to develop his or her identity from a lower to a higher plane of morality—from the immoral David at the beginning to the later David who shows signs of a moral awakening; from David's anger to Lucy's forgiveness and reconciliation; from David's apathy at the beginning to Bev's care for people and animals—each reader applying the narrative to her or his own personality and circumstances. As Kearney says, literature is "an open-ended invitation to ethical involvement" (Kearney 2002: 156).

Religious overtones

David is not a religious man, yet he needs vestiges of religion to work through his crises. Derek Attridge, in a chapter on *Disgrace*, also commented on this:

> In his reaching for a register that escapes the terminology of the administered society Coetzee has often turned to religious discourse, and there is a continuity among several of his characters who find that, although they apparently have no orthodox beliefs, they cannot talk about their lives without such language. (Attridge 2005: 180)

David says to Mr Isaacs, Melanie's father, when the latter confronts him with the demands of God: "As for God, I am not a believer, so I will have to translate what you call God and God's wishes into my own terms" (172). He then proceeds to elaborate on his way of translating religious concepts: he accepts the punishment meted out to him for the wrongs he committed, he realises that he has fallen into a state of disgrace and tries to accept disgrace as his state of being (172). The way in which David reverts to religious language during his visit to the Isaacs family is striking. When he meets Melanie's attractive sister and is filled with erotic desire, he thinks, apparently with guilt and shame: "*God save me ... what am I doing here?*" (164). When Isaacs invites him for a meal, it sounds like an invitation to Holy Communion: "Break bread with us" (167). David's words of greeting when he arrives that evening, link up with the invitation: "'I brought an offering,' he says, and holds out a bottle of wine" (168). When he meets Mrs Isaacs, and notices the strong bond between husband and wife, his thoughts are clad in Biblical words: "*And ye shall be as one flesh*" (169). His acknowledgement of guilt, his remorse and his asking for pardon, all have a strong religious flavour. As a "post-religious" person, he cannot pray, but he goes so far as to kneel before Melanie's mother and sister to ask for their forgiveness. The evening with the Isaacs family is structured like a religious ritual; David clearly feels the need for such a ritual to work through his shameful past.

There are also other religious echoes in *Disgrace*, reminiscent of sacrificial rituals, the cleansing of sins and the establishment of social justice. For instance, the slaughtering of the two sheep at Petrus's feast to mark the dawning of a new era fits in with the ritualistic language in the rest of the novel; the cleaning of the dam by Petrus, with the help of David, is symbolic of an individual and communal cleansing process. Of central importance, furthermore, are the concepts of "disgrace" and "grace", which reverberate with religious associations. They are ingrained in the novel; they help David to make sense of his bewildering situation. As mentioned above, he realises that he lives in a state of disgrace and accepts it as a just punishment for his disgraceful behaviour. Disgraceful behaviour is, however, not limited to David; disgrace envelops the colonial past and is already part of the new discourse; variations of rape abound. Paradise has been lost irrevocably, and humanity has fallen from grace. Inherent in the human state of being, Coetzee implies, is its disgrace—which includes the shamefulness of people's conduct as well as their being subjected to physical decay and humiliating death.

Different connotations of the concept "disgrace" should be noted here. It could refer to bad ("disgraceful") behaviour as well as to the condition of having lost people's respect ("fallen from grace"). Both meanings are applicable in the novel; for instance, David's disgrace is the result of his disgraceful behaviour. However, the disgrace of the situation is not always a just reflection of the disgrace of the deed—on the contrary, sometimes the innocent suffer. In *Disgrace*, animals are included in the humiliating state of being, and David learns to sympathise with dogs sharing in the disgrace of dying:

> They flatten their ears, they droop their tails, as they too feel the disgrace of dying; locking their legs, they have to be pulled or pushed or carried over the

> threshold. On the table some snap wildly left and right, some whine plaintively; none will look straight at the needle in Bev's hand, which they somehow know is going to harm them terribly. (143)

Disgrace is linked to humiliation and shame—but feelings of shame are often not proportionate to the shamefulness of the deed involved. It is significant that shame does not necessarily cling to the person who committed a disgraceful action; often the shame is transmitted to the victim. That is especially the case with rape—the rape of Lucy being a striking example. The rapists are not ashamed of the harm they inflicted; but Lucy, the innocent victim, has feelings of shame. She wants to hide her face:

> Because of the disgrace. Because of the shame. That is what their visitors have achieved; that is what they have done to this confident, modern young woman. Like a stain the story is spreading across the district. (115)

Disgraceful behaviour is like an infectious disease, spreading its effects of disgrace and shame. The "stains" of the colonial past and the ensuing deeds of the rapists have now infected Lucy as well, so that she has become part of an all-enveloping communal narrative of guilt and shame. The crucial question is whether the narrative of disgrace can be counterbalanced by a narrative of grace, spreading its effects like an "infectious" healing. How can grace make its entrance into a history so fundamentally polluted?

For a religious person, all earthly grace is initiated by a God of grace, granting unmerited favours to humanity. David and Lucy have to translate this theological idea of grace to make sense of their lives in their post-religious state. David's progress with his opera is also not unrelated to grace, as Attridge points out:

> Although he expends great effort on his musical composition, it seems to emerge, when it does so, in a form which he feels is worth preserving, without his willing it (and the word *blessedly* suggests that the religious register is not inappropriate here). (Attridge 2005: 183)

David's caring for the sick and dead animals is also an example of grace entering the world of the novel. The animals cannot help themselves, neither can they reward David for his kindness; they are totally dependent on his mercy. When a person in disgrace shows mercy to other beings sharing his disgraceful condition, grace makes its appearance.

Lucy's response to her rape is the prime example of grace entering the novel. Looking at the event in itself, Lucy is the innocent victim of criminal men. What happened to her is a disgrace. However, Lucy, as mentioned before, chooses to link the event to a history of injustice in the country. Although she insists that her decision has nothing to do with religious abstractions such as guilt and salvation, the story of her rape recalls a central theme of many religions (for instance, in Judaism, Christianity and most African religions): the vicarious sacrifice of the innocent (human or animal) to remove the guilt of society and propitiate God/the gods. It is significant that, just before the appearance of the rapists, David elaborates on scapegoats and the present-day need to "cleanse the city without divine help" (91). Lucy's action is a modern translation of the age-old story of the innocent scapegoat. Through deliberately choosing to accept her rape as punishment for the collective guilt of Europeans in Africa, and not insisting on her individual innocence, balance is restored; grace enters the scene; peace can be found.

Through Lucy, grace is also transmitted to David. In an interview with David Attwell, Coetzee distinguishes between "cynicism" and "grace": "Cynicism: the denial of any ultimate basis for values. Grace: a condition in which the truth can be told clearly, without blindness" (Coetzee 1992: 392). Coetzee here refers back to an essay that he regards as "pivotal" in his own development, and which is included in the same book: an essay entitled "Confession and Double Thoughts: Tolstoy, Rousseau, Dostoevsky" (Coetzee 1992: 251–293). In this essay, Coetzee mentions Dostoevsky's belief that true confession comes from "faith and grace" (Coetzee 1992: 291). In his discussion of Tolstoy's *Anna Karenina*, Coetzee suggests the possibility of truth emerging not from self-examination "but in illumination from outside", and, as an example, he refers to "the sudden illumination of a peasant's words" in Tolstoy's work. One is reminded here of David, calling his daughter "a peasant" (*Disgrace* 217), and of the associations of her name with illumination. More and more, as the story unfolds, Lucy becomes a vehicle of grace through her revelation to David of ethical values.

Towards the end of the narrative Lucy makes a statement with strong religious overtones:

> Perhaps that is what I must learn to accept. To start at ground level. With nothing. Not with nothing but. With nothing. No cards, no weapons, no property, no rights, no dignity. (205)

This laying down of the old desires to begin a new life, this spiritual rebirth, echoes many of the central thoughts of Buddhism and Christianity. We also have the Hindu dance of Shiva here, with new life emerging from the destruction of the old. In a time of trauma, *Disgrace* seems to suggest, one needs a religion to work through it—if conventional religions have lost their meaning, one needs to create a modern adaptation of the fundamental, age-old concepts embodied in religion.

The great archetypes of the mind

Closely connected to the ethical and religious aspects of the novel, is the focus on what David calls "the great archetypes of the mind" (22). David is a Romantic, like the poets whom he admires, Wordsworth and Byron. The typical Romantic is ill at ease in the world, painfully conscious of its transience and imperfection, and is filled with an intense longing for higher ideals, for that which is timeless and perfect. David is obsessed with the idea of perfect beauty, but the other two concepts conventionally linked to beauty, namely goodness and truth, are also important to him. (One is reminded of Lionel Ruby's remark: "The history of philosophy may be regarded as the record of man's search for adequate analytical definitions of the key terms in human discourse, words such as 'truth', 'beauty' and 'goodness'" (Ruby 1968: 44)). Another idea that plays a prominent role, especially towards the end of the novel, is the idea of love. David's discourse is filled with concepts that have dominated Western philosophy, mainly derived from three traditions: Judaism (especially the concept of justice), ancient Greek philosophy (beauty, truth and goodness) and Christianity (love).

Note that David broods on ideas crucial to Western philosophy and ethics, but shows no interest in the ethical system of Petrus. He is unable to enter the discourse of the black man, unable to create a work of literature that transcends Western views of the world, and so sticks to his opera about the English poet Byron. The concept of *ubuntu*, central in the ethical system of Africa, which was discussed in chapter 1, could for instance have illuminated David's ethics and enriched his creative work.

Truth is not portrayed as a single, absolute concept, but rather as truths of discourse, narrative truths. David and Petrus are caught up in their contrasting narratives; but Lucy has reached a higher level of truth, an awareness of both narratives, which makes it possible for her to link the two and bring about reconciliation. Linked to "truth" is the idea of justice—we have noticed that David's and Petrus's different ideas about the historical truth of South Africa lead to different ideas of justice.

Of the timeless ideas that determine David's arguments and conclusions, the most important are beauty, goodness and love. David is initially attracted by physical beauty—of Soraya, and especially of Melanie—and he wants to possess it. His desire for taking possession lacks a moral dimension; it takes little notice of the desire of the possessed. David's analysis with his students of Byron's portrayal of Lucifer leads to an indirect analysis of his own character: "He [Lucifer] does what he feels like. He doesn't care if it's good or bad. He just does it." To this remark by Melanie's boyfriend, who attends the class and whose comments clearly have a bearing on David's behaviour towards Melanie, David responds:

> Exactly. Good or bad, he just does it. He doesn't act on principle but on impulse … His madness was not of the head, but of the heart … He is exactly what he calls himself: a *thing*, that is, a monster. Finally, Byron will suggest, it will not be possible to love him, not in the deeper, more human sense of the word. He will be condemned to solitude. (33–34)

This indirect analysis of the Lucifer side in him must have been alarming to David; he too, like Byron's Lucifer, is unable to form lasting human relationships, and his final destination seems to be solitude. This sombre prospect may have been a motivation for David to search for an alternative way of life.

It should also be noted that David is never a complete monster; there are sides to his personality which leave room for positive change. He is probably right when he maintains that, in the affair with Melanie, "there was something generous that was doing its best to flower" (89): his desire for Melanie was linked to an appreciation of her beauty. Furthermore, he has his moments of tender and protective feelings towards her: "Poor little bird, he thinks, whom I have held against my breast" (32). In spite of his self-righteousness before the university's investigation committee, he sometimes confronts his own guilt: "No more than a child! What am I doing?" and "Melanie, who barely comes to his shoulder. Unequal: how can he deny that?" (53). In an inner dialogue he has with Melanie's father, David condemns himself in the ethical language of Mr Isaacs: "Your daughter lost respect for me weeks ago, and with good reason … I am the worm in the apple" (37).

In his relationship with Melanie, David falls into the trap which he mentions to his students: "The great archetypes of the mind, pure ideas, find themselves usurped by mere sense-images" (22). He was so enticed by Melanie's physical beauty that he lost track of the pure and absolute idea of beauty. On the other hand, it is impossible for humans to be totally absorbed by ideas and forsake the physical world. David has to find a way to link the ideal and the real world; he has to find answers to the great question which he formulates thus to his students:

> Yet we cannot live our daily lives in a realm of pure ideas, cocooned from sense-experience. The question is not, How can we keep the imagination pure, protected from the onslaughts of reality? The question has to be, Can we find a way for the two to coexist? (22)

David's views on beauty change dramatically in the course of the narrative. He learns to distinguish between archetypal beauty and physical beauty; he also learns to link archetypal beauty to goodness, the second archetype of the mind to be discussed here. Furthermore, these two pure ideas, archetypal beauty and goodness, are "brought down" into the reality of practical, everyday life by Lucy, and David learns to appreciate what he now sees in his daughter.

Let us briefly trace the development of David's views on beauty after his fall from grace at the university. His contact with Bev has a marked influence on him. Bev is strikingly unattractive, a total contrast to Melanie, and when he meets her, he thinks to himself that "he does not like women who make no effort to be attractive" (72). Yet immediately thereafter he reproaches himself, admitting that "his mind has become a refuge for old thoughts". His way of thinking about female beauty is one of the old thoughts not fitting for him any more. Bev, in her compassion for needy humans and animals, has an inner beauty which David learns to appreciate.

It comes as a surprise to the reader when the relationship between David and Bev acquires a sexual dimension—surprising that the seemingly virtuous and happily married Bev is the one to lure David into a sexual encounter. Perhaps, though, Bev was less interested in sex than in showing compassion for David; the event is linked to her care for animals, because David is a poor old dog too. It is significant that, when they get together after the first sexual meeting, the sexual aspect falls away, Bev strokes his hair and speaks comforting words to him: "You mustn't worry … Bill and I will look after [Lucy]" (162). Note that she still sees Bill as her husband and companion; she has no intention of leaving him for the sake of an adulterous relationship with David.

Even more surprising is the fact that David is willing to be drawn into a sexual encounter with the physically unattractive Bev. What a contrast to his relationship with the beautiful Melanie! David thinks about the contrast himself: "After the sweet young flesh of Melanie Isaacs, this is what I have come to" (150). In spite of his feeling of degradation, he does not despise Bev, but feels rather sympathetic towards her: "Well, let poor Bev Shaw go home and do some singing too. And let him stop calling her poor Bev Shaw. If she is poor, he is bankrupt" (150). As the story develops, his admiration for Bev keeps growing, and he is ultimately completely drawn into her care for the animals. Increasingly, he comes to the realisation that the ugly Bev is doing something beautiful.

The shift in David's attention from beautiful young woman to mature women with an inner beauty is also suggested by the change of focus in the opera he is writing. He lets go of his original idea of writing about Teresa as the passionate young lover of Byron and decides to write about her as "a dumpy little widow" (181). Teresa has now lost her physical attraction; her claim to interest lies in her faithful love of the deceased Byron. Through her love she manages, in David's opera, to bring Byron back to life; through her steadfast love, she is "supporting him, saving him from going down" (183). David has become more interested in faithful, life-giving love than in youthful beauty and passion.

Near the end of the narrative, David makes one last attempt to contact Melanie, but it leads to a pitiful failure. After this failure, he is ready for some momentous conclusions on the nature of beauty and goodness. Although he does not condone Lucy's response to her rape and cannot emulate the completeness of her self-sacrifice, he comes to admire her for her strength of character. In a discussion about her attitude towards the baby she is expecting, Lucy remarks:

> Love will grow—one can trust Mother Nature for that. I am determined to be a good mother, David. A good mother and a good person. You should try to be a good person too. (216)

Although David doubts his own ability to be a good man, he admires the ideal: "A good person. Not a bad resolution to make, in dark times" (216).

Note that this discussion comes near the end of the novel, and is part of the set of "conclusions" to which the "argument" of the narrative leads. Goodness is here linked to love; it is also, in the following pages, linked to beauty. David watches Lucy, working in the garden, without her being aware of him. He notices the backs of her knees, "the least beautiful part of a woman's body" (217), but then adds compassion to this cold aesthetic perspective, and concludes that it is also "the most endearing" part.

On the next page, Lucy in her garden becomes part of an idyllic setting, a moment when timeless beauty seems to take on an earthly form:

> There is a moment of utter stillness which he would wish prolonged for ever: the gentle sun, the stillness of mid-afternoon, bees busy in a field of flowers; and at the centre of the picture a young woman, *das ewig Weibliche*, lightly pregnant, in a straw sunhat. A scene ready-made for a Sargent or a Bonnard. City boys like him; but even city boys can recognize beauty when they see it, can have their breath taken away. (218)

David has now moved from darkness to light, from Melanie to Lucy. He has learned to appreciate a beauty radically different from the beauty of the senses only—the beauty which drew him to Melanie—and to appreciate a beauty based on the ethical values of goodness and love. Through her goodness, Lucy attains the beauty of an inner harmony: the willingness to face what she knows should be done and the strength to do it. She has reached "wholeness", her inner conflicts have been resolved, and therefore she is "solid in her existence" (217). Note that Lucy's beauty is placed within a specific context, that of a garden on a farm where she belongs; it is only in that context that her wholeness makes sense.

"When the Absolute falls into water, it becomes a fish", said Bernard Bosanquet (quoted in Hoernlé 1924: 176). Usually we make a distinction between the two opposites, the absolute and the relative. That which is absolute, is fixed, unchanging, timeless and universal; whereas that which is relative, continually changes as it is determined and defined by different contexts. Bosanquet paradoxically combines the two opposites; in his statement, the Absolute remains true to itself, yet takes on the form ideal for the context in which it is placed. In *Disgrace*, Bosanquet's Absolute Beauty falls, not into water, but on a farm; it becomes, not a fish, but an adaptable female farmer. David ultimately learns to value this kind of beauty, inextricably bound to goodness and inner wholeness, and to appreciate it without attempting to overpower it, as he did with Melanie.

The third absolute to be discussed here is that of love, a concept central in Christianity, but also important in many other religions and philosophical systems. Note that Lucy's decision to love her child is based not on spontaneous feelings, but on an act of will. She responds to hate with a determination to love; she manages to rise above the natural response of reciprocal hate and reaches a spiritual height attained by few.

Love by definition is relative, in the sense that it is bound to relations; yet there are unchanging elements present in all loving relationships. In *Disgrace*, the basic paradox of all love is examined: the paradox of attachment versus *Lösung* (letting go) (142). David has always had difficulty in grasping this central paradox of love. With Soraya there was little attachment, yet he found it hard to let her go; with Melanie there was more attachment, but also more possessiveness; most of all, he was attached to his daughter Lucy, but his way of caring for her was to try and control her life and prevent her from creating her life story as she deemed right.

Only at the end of the novel does David manage to experience love, love towards dying dogs: "He has learned by now … to concentrate all his attention on the animal they are killing, giving it what he no longer has difficulty in calling by its proper name: love" (219). David has to learn the hard task of giving up the loved animals, of handing them over to death. He becomes especially attached to one dog, one that appreciates the music of his opera. The novel ends with David's bringing this dog to a merciful death, "bearing him in his arms like a lamb" (220). As well as the attachment, David has learned the *Lösung* proper to love. Compared with the magnitude of Lucy's sacrifice, David's sacrifice is small, perhaps pathetic; he is still unable to love humans, and can only love dying dogs in a situation where he is in control. Yet for someone with his self-centred nature this may be the first step towards a more ethical life. In the words of Charles Sarvan:

> Lurie's act of giving up the dog is symbolic of relinquishment, of a surrendering of attachment, attachment and desire from which, according to the Buddha, come suffering and sorrow. In giving himself up, and in giving himself *to*, Lurie finds himself. 'But whoever … overcomes his selfish cravings, his sorrows fall away from him, like drops of water from a lotus flower' (*Dhammapada*). (Sarvan 2004: 29)

The focus in this chapter, as well as in the whole book, has been on the healing of the traumatic wounds of individuals and society. The way to healing, *Disgrace* suggests, lies in the return to the great archetypes of the mind, especially beauty, goodness and love. Even readers who do not agree with all the aspects of our interpretation of *Disgrace* in this chapter, should not discard the importance of these timeless ethical concepts to obtain harmony for individuals and society—the importance of beauty based on goodness, and of love that cares but lets go. The written text should lead to the rewriting of our lives. The great Absolutes should fall into the waters of the readers, changing into different fish as they enter the world.

REFERENCES

Abraham, N & Torok, M. 1994. *The Shell and the Kernel, Renewals of Psychoanalysis, Volume 1.* Chicago: University of Chicago Press.

Ackermann, Denise. 2003. On the Language of Lament. In Denise Ackermann: *After the Locusts. Letters from a Landscape of Faith*, 98–128. Grand Rapids, Michigan/Cambridge, UK: William B Eerdmans.

ANC News Briefing. 2000. Mediaracism-ANC. Sapa, Johannesburg, 5 April. http://www.anc.org.za/anc/newsbrief/2000/news0406.txt

Apfelbaum, Erika. 2002. Restoring Lives Shattered by Collective Violence. In C N van der Merwe & R Wolfswinkel: *Telling Wounds. Narrative, Trauma & Memory—Working through the South African Armed Conflicts of the 20th Century*. Stellenbosch: Van Schaik Content Solutions. 9–20.

Attridge, Derek. 2005. *J M Coetzee and the Ethics of Reading.* Chicago: University of Chicago Press, and Scottsville: University of Kwazulu-Natal Press.

Attridge, Derek & Peter D McDonald (eds). 2002. J M Coetzee's *Disgrace*. Special issue, *Interventions: International Journal of Postcolonial Studies* 4 (3).

B'hahn, Carmella. 2002. *Mourning has Broken: Learning from the Wisdom of Adversity.* Bath: Crucible Publishers.

Beveridge, A. 1998. On the Origins of Post-traumatic Stress Disorder. In D Black (ed), *Psychological Trauma: A Developmental Approach*, 3–9.

Blanchot, Maurice. 1982. *The Space of Literature* (orig. *L'Espace littéraure*, 1955). Translated by Ann Smock. Lincoln/London: University of Nebraska Press.

Brand, G. 2002. *Speaking of a Fabulous Ghost. Contributions to Philosophical Theology,* Vol. 7. New York/Frankfurt: Peter Lang.

Breuer, J & Freud, S. 1936. *Studies in Hysteria.* (trans. A A Brill). New York & Washington: Nervous and Mental Disease Publishing Company.

Brison, S. 2002. *Aftermath: Violence and the Remaking of the Self.* Princeton: Princeton University Press.

Burger, Willie. 2001. The Past is Another Country: Narrative, Identity and the Achievement of Moral Consciousness in Afrikaans Historiographical Fiction. *Stilet,* 13 (2) 79–91.

Carr, David. 1997. Narrative and the Real World: An Argument for Continuity. In L P Hinchman & S K Hinchman (eds), *Memory, Identity, Community. The*

Idea of Narrative in the Human Sciences, 7–25. New York: New York University Press.

Caruth, C. 1995. *Unclaimed Experience: Trauma, Narrative, and History.* Baltimore: Johns Hopkins University Press.

Coetzee, J M. 1988. *White Writing. On the Culture of Letters in South Africa.* London/New Haven: Yale University Press.

—. 1992. *Doubling the Point. Essays and Interviews.* Cambridge, Mass/London: Harvard University Press.

—. 1999. *Disgrace*. London: Secker & Warburg.

—. 2003. *Elizabeth Costello*. London: Secker & Warburg.

Coetzee, P H & A P J Roux (eds). 1998. *Philosophy from Africa: A Text with Readings*. Johannesburg/London: International Thomson Publishing.

Delbo, Charlotte. 1990. *Days and Memory* (orig. *La mémoire et les jours*, 1985). *Translated by Rosette Lamont.* Marlboro, Vermont: Marlboro Press.

Felman, Shoshana. 1995. Education and Crisis, or the Vicissitudes of Teaching. In Cathy Caruth (ed) *Trauma: Explorations in Memory*, 13–60. Baltimore/London: Johns Hopkins University Press.

Field, Sean. 2006. Beyond "Healing": Trauma, Oral History and Regeneration. *Oral History*, 34 (1) 31–42.

Frankl, Viktor. 1985 (orig. 1946). *Man's Search for Meaning.* Translated by Ilse Lasch. New York: Pocket Books.

Friedlander, S. (ed). 1992. *Probing the Limits of Representation: Nazism and the Final Solution*. Cambridge MA: Harvard University Press.

Fussel, P. 1975. *The Great War and Modern Memory.* New York: Oxford University Press.

Gagiano, Annie. 2004. "Racial" characterisation in the apartheid-period and post-apartheid writings of J M Coetzee. In N Distiller & M Steyn, *Under Construction. "Race" and Identity in South Africa today*, 38–47. Sandton: Heinemann.

Gobodo-Madikizela, Pumla. 2003. *A Human Being Died That Night.* Cape Town: David Philip.

Graham, L V. 2003. Reading the Unspeakable: Rape in J M Coetzee's *Disgrace*. *Journal of Southern African Studies*, 29 (2) 433–444.

Hall, Stuart. 1994. Cultural Identity and Diaspora. In P Williams & L Chrisman (eds), *Colonial Discourse and Post-colonial Theory. A Reader*, 392–403. New York: Harvester Wheatsleaf.

Herman, J. 1992. *Trauma and Recovery: The Aftermath of Violence, From Domestic Abuse to Political Terror.* New York: Basic Books.

Hoernlé, R F A. 1924. *Idealism as a Philosophical Doctrine.* London: Hodder & Stoughton.

Iannone, Carol. 2005. Post-apartheid in Black and White. *The American Conservative,* February 14. http://www.amconmag.com/2005_02_14/article2.html

Jung, G G. 1968. *The Archetypes and the Collective Unconscious.* Second edition. Translated by R F C Hull. London: Routledge.

Kearney, Richard. 2002. *On Stories. Thinking in Action.* London/New York: Routledge.

Kermode, Frank. 1967. *The Sense of an Ending.* New York: Oxford University Press.

Kernberg, O F. 2003. The Management of Affect Storms in Psychoanalytic Psychotherapy of Borderline Patients. *Journal of the American Psychoanalytic Association (APA)*, 51 (2) 517–545.

Kluger, Ruth. 2004. *Landscapes of Memory. A Holocaust Girlhood Remembered.* London: Bloomsbury.

Kossew, Sue. 2003. The Politics of Shame and Redemption in J.M. Coetzee's *Disgrace. Research in African Literatures,* 34 (2) 155–162.

Kristeva, Julia. 1989 (orig. 1987). *Black Sun. Depression and Melancholia.* Translated by Leon S Roudiez. New York: Columbia University Press.

LaCapra, Dominick. 1994. *Representing the Holocaust. History, Theory, Trauma.* Ithaca/London: Cornell University Press.

—. 2001. *Writing History, Writing Trauma.* Baltimore: Johns Hopkins University Press.

Langer, L. 1991. *Holocaust Testimonies: The Ruins of Memory.* New Haven: Yale University Press.

Laub, D. 1992. An Event Without a Witness: Truth, Testimony, and Survival. In S Felman & D Laub, *Testimony: Crises of Witnessing in Literature, Psychoanalysis and History*. New York and London: Routledge.

Laub, D & S Lee. 2003. Thanatos and Massive Psychic Trauma: The Impact of the Death Instinct on Knowing, Remembering, and Forgetting, *Journal of the American Psychoanalytic Association (APA),* 51 (2) 433–463.

Levi, Primo. 1985. *If Not Now, When?* New York: Penguin.

—. n.d. *If This is a Man* and *The Truce.* Kettering, Northants: Abacus.

Leys, R. 2000. *Trauma: A Genealogy.* Chicago: University of Chicago Press.

MacIntyre, Alasdair. 1981. *After Virtue. A Study in Moral Theory.* Notre Dame, Ind.: University of Notre Dame Press.

Maclear, Kyo. 1999. *Beclouded Visions: Hiroshima-Nagasaki and the Art of Witness.* Albany: State University of New York Press.

—. 2003. The Limits of Vision: *Hiroshima Mon Amour* and the Subversion of Representation. In Ana Douglass & Thomas A Vogler (eds), *Witness and Memory: The Discourse of Trauma.* New York: Routledge.

Marais, Mike. 2000. The possibility of ethical action: J. M. Coetzee's *Disgrace*. *Scrutiny2*, 5 (1) 57–63.

—. 2003. Reading against race: J M Coetzee's *Disgrace*, Justin Cartwright's *White Lightning* and Ivan Vladislavic's *The Restless Supermarket*. *Journal of Literary Studies* 19 (3–4) 271–289.

Moreiras, A. 1996. The Aura of Testimonio. In G M Gugelberger (ed), *The Real Thing: Testimonial Discourse and Latin America*. Durham, North Carolina: Duke University Press.

Murphy, J S. 2004. Past Irony: Trauma and the Historical Turn in *Fragments* and *The Swimming-Pool Library*. *Literature & History*, 13 (1) 58–75.

Nouwen, Henri. 1972. *The Wounded Healer*. New York/London: Doubleday.

Poyner, Jayne. 2000. Truth and Reconciliation in J M Coetzee's *Disgrace*. *Scrutiny 2*, 5 (2) 67–77.

Reisner, S. 2002. Staging the Unspeakable. *Psychosocial Notebook*, 3: 9–30. Geneva: International Organisation for Migration.

Ricœur, Paul. 1983. Can Fictional Narratives Be True? *Analecta Husserliana*, 14: 3–19.

Ricœur, Paul. 1988 (orig. 1985). *Time and Narrative, Volume 3*. Translated by Kathleen Blamey and David Pellauer. Chicago/London; University of Chicago Press.

—. 1991. Life: A Story in Search of a Narrator. In Mario Valdés (ed), *A Ricœur Reader: Reflection and Imagination*, 425–437. Toronto: University of Toronto Press.

—. 1992 (orig. 1990). *Oneself as another*. Translated by Kathleen Blamey. Chicago/London: University of Chicago Press.

—. 2004. *Memory, History, Forgetting*. Translated by Kathleen Blamey and David Pellauer. Chicago/London: University of Chicago Press.

Robson, Kathryn. 2004. *Writing Wounds. The Inscription of Trauma in Post-1968 French Women's Life-Writing*. Amsterdam/New York: Rodopi.

Rossouw, P J. 2001. Die bevrydingstryd. Biblioterapie as kognitiewe herstrukturering by slagoffers van gewapende konflik in Suidelike Afrika. In C N Van der Merwe & R Wolfswinkel, *De Helende Kracht van Literatuur. Over Nederlands en Suid-Afrikaans Oorlogsproza,* 33–60. Haarlem: In de Knipscheer.

Ruby, Lionel. 1968. *The Art of Making Sense*. London: Angus & Robertson.

Sachs, Albie. 1998 (paper originally presented in 1989). Preparing Ourselves for Freedom. In D Attridge & R Jolly (eds), *Writing South Africa. Literature, Apartheid and Democracy, 1970–1995*. 239–248. Cambridge UK: Cambridge University Press.

Sarvan, Charles. 2004. *Disgrace:* A path to grace? *World Literature Today*, January–April, 26–29.

Schnell, Lise. 2000. The Language of Grief. *Vermont Quarterly*, Fall 2000, 25–29.

Sontag, Susan. 2004. *Regarding the Pain of Others*. London: Penguin Books.

US Committee for Refugees. 2000. *World Refugee Survey.* Washington, DC: Immigration and Refugee Services of America.

Van Alphen, Ernst. 1999. Symptoms of Discursivity: Experience, Memory, and Trauma. In Mieke Bal, Jonathan Crewe & Leo Spitzer (eds), *Acts of Memory. Cultural Recall in the Present*, 24–38. Hanover/London, University Press of New England.

Van der Kolk, Bessel A. 1989. The Compulsion to Repeat the Trauma: Re-enactment, Revictimization, and Masochism. *Psychiatric Clinics of North America*, 12 (2) 389–411.

—. 1996. Trauma and Memory. In B Van der Kolk, A C McFarlane & L Weisaeth (eds), *Traumatic Stress*. New York: Guilford Press. 279–302.

Van der Kolk, Bessel A & O Van der Hart. 1995. The Intrusive Past: The Flexibility of Memory and the Engraving of Trauma. In C Caruth (ed), *Trauma. Explorations in Memory*, 158–182. Baltimore/London: Johns Hopkins University Press.

Van der Merwe, C N. 1994. *Breaking Barriers: Stereotypes and the Changing of Values in Afrikaans Writing, 1875–1990.* Amsterdam: Rodopi.

Van Heerden, Etienne. 1998. *Kikuyu* (originally *Kikoejoe*, 1996.) Translated by Catherine Knox. Cape Town: Kwela Books.

Viljoen, Shaun. 2001. Non-racialism remains a fiction: From Richard Rive's *Buckingham Palace: District Six* to K. Sello Duiker's *The quiet violence of dreams. The English Academy Review,* 18: 46–53.

Wiesel, Elie. 1968. *Legends of Our Time.* New York: Holt, Rinehart & Winston.

—. 1977. Art and Culture After the Holocaust. In Eva Fleischner (ed.) *Auschwitz: Beginning of a New Era?* New York: Ktav Publishing House. 405.

Wigren, Jodie. 1994. Narrative Completion in the Treatment of Trauma. *Psychotherapy*, 31 (3) 415–423.

INDEX